Teaching That Works

Strategies FROM Scripture FOR Classrooms Today

Cliff Schimmels

STANDARD
PUBLISHING

Cincinnati, Ohio

Cover by Howe Design
Standard Publishing, Cincinnati, Ohio
A division of Standex International Corporation

06   05   04   03   02   01   00   99   5   4   3   2   1

ISBN 0-7847-1052-X

Contents

To Teachers Everywhere

I write this book as an expression of my gratitude for all of your efforts. Whether you are a professional teacher or a church volunteer; whether you teach five year olds or eighty year olds, you are the salt of the earth. I owe a debt to you for your hard work and commitment.

I can attest to the results of your teaching. I myself am a product of Mrs. Simmons, who taught me how to find subjects and verbs so that I could make sentences; of Mrs. Townsend, who taught about exotic places such as Ukraine and China so that I could dream of traveling someday; of Mrs. Paris, who made me memorize the books of the Bible in order so that I can find the passages I need to read; of Mrs. Smith, who in a one-hour-a-week Sunday school class taught me to have enough confidence in myself to write a book.

I can attest to the results of your teaching in the lives of others. I teach at a university, and every day I associate with the young adults who have come through your classes.

Someone has taught them well. They have a great supply of knowledge. They have learned how to study and learn. They are courteous and responsible. Most importantly, they have learned to be sensitive, caring, and cheerful. They have learned to rejoice with those who rejoice and mourn with those who mourn.

During my twenty-five years of teaching young adults at the university, I have become an outspoken fan of teachers—public school teachers, Sunday school teachers, vacation Bible school workers, children's church leaders, youth directors. I see the results of your work in living examples, and my life is richer because of what you do. This book is a statement of my appreciation.

My theme is simple: *The Bible is a great educational methods textbook.* I teach a class called Teaching Methods. To prepare for that assignment, I study the field. I read the latest journals. I attend seminars and workshops. I study the research findings. I learn to use the latest terms such as cooperative learning, whole-language approach, age-appropriate instruction, multisensory teaching, learning styles, computer-assisted instruction, divergent questions, and hands-on learning.

I enjoy this study, and I find it profitable. I sit in my office, read the newest ideas from the educational scientists, and say, "What a great insight! I can use that. Other teachers can use that." Then I open my Bible and find the very same insight in practice two thousand years ago. It is not new at all; we have just rediscovered it. A frequent repetition of that experience has convinced me that I should begin my study of teaching in the Bible. For years, people have asked, "What do the current educators have to offer to the field of Bible teaching?" I think it is time to propose the second question, "What does the Bible have to offer to current educators?"

Of course, my idea is not an original. Through the years, some excellent educators have written books about Jesus, the Master Teacher, which I have found invaluable in my study of education. This book is an update and an expansion because it includes discussions of some other great teachers presented in the Bible. I have not written an exhaustive investigation of all the teaching methods employed by the people in the Old and New Testaments. Instead I have written only an introduction, a cursory discussion of a few of the examples.

My purpose in writing this book is also simple: *I want to encourage you to study your Bible.* As a good teacher, you want to get better. That's one of the ironies of this calling. Good teachers are always eager to find ways to improve. You are always searching for new ideas, new techniques, new strategies. I suggest that you begin your search by reading your Bible. Learn about teaching strategies during your daily devotions. Then if you are so moved, you can consult the current educational literature just to confirm your findings.

I call the concepts "methods," realizing that the word may be a bit misleading. Sometimes we limit the meaning to tips, clues, tricks of the trade. I use it in a broader sense. Methods are the process by which I get my mind around the purpose and content of my lesson so I can be the most effective instructor possible.

After forty years on the teacher's side of the desk, I have come to understand that teaching well is not some mysterious, scientific process that can be accomplished only by the multitalented and specifically gifted. Instead, teaching well is taking care of the little things: telling the students the purpose of the class before the lesson begins, using a little story to illustrate a point, finding an appropriate prop on which to hang an abstract idea, visiting a sick student at home, or sending a card of congratulations. Nothing epic. Nothing astounding—just the simple little techniques that we can all perform. But when we put those little things together, we just might become the agents that God uses to change the lives and the direction of eternity for those people who sit in our classes every week.

Chapter 1

The Stricter Judgment

James 3:1

"We who teach will be judged more strictly."

James 3:1

"Wherever we go, we cast a shadow as teachers, and people look at us with different expectations."

11

 Why are you a teacher? In straightforward language James 3:1 warns, "Not many of you should presume to be teachers, my brothers, because you know that we who teach will be judged more strictly."

Whether you are a church volunteer or a full-time professional, the question is the same: Why do you teach? Why do you put yourself through the agony, the tears, the emotional roller coaster, the hard work, the hours of commitment just to be judged more strictly?

To help you ponder that question, consider the following list of ten statements. You might be a teacher if . . .

10. Your Bible looks like a file cabinet.

9. No matter how pressing the business deal, you are never more than a thought away from the lesson plan in progress.

8. "Teaching supplies" is a line item in your personal budget.

7. You talk to yourself.

6. You collect what other people call garbage—useful teaching tools like Popsicle sticks, nut cups, and empty milk or egg cartons.

5. You can't watch television without thinking that you should be studying instead.

4. Your emotional state is determined by whether or not your ten year olds listened to you that day.

12

3. You have been known to wear two different-colored socks to church on Sunday morning.

2. Your favorite days of the year are Christmas, Easter, and the days new quarterlies arrive.

1. The sweetest music in the world is to hear someone say, "Dear Jesus, I'm a sinner!"

If six or more of these statements apply to you, you just might be an incurable teacher. You have accepted the heartaches, the frustrations, the anxieties, the rewards—and the stricter judgment. You are reading this book because you are serious about teaching.

I am serious about teaching, too. I have been teaching for forty years—forty years of not sleeping well the night before a lesson; forty years of fearing the lesson plan will bomb in the middle of class; forty years of having some student make some comment that takes me by surprise; forty years of visiting the students at home, writing cards, and making telephone calls; forty years of watching students grow; forty years of hearing from them years later with news both good and bad; forty years of celebrating the call and actually feeling sorry for the people who aren't teachers.

I've also spent forty years pondering what James meant with his warning about the stricter judgment. I still don't know for sure, but after all those years I have confirmed some principles of the enterprise that help me get a clearer picture.

Teaching is a calling.

"Good teachers are born, not made," people tell me every day. They know that I teach teachers, and they want to see my response. I agree with them. Of course good teachers are born. In his list of gifts in Romans 12, Paul assures us that teaching is one of those special abilities given to us by God. We don't choose to be teachers, God chooses us! But some of us may take a bit longer than others to discover that we have this gift.

However, just because we are given the ability to teach doesn't mean that our skill is fully developed. We still need to grow. Great piano players are born, too, but Van Cliburn still had to take lessons. Great tennis players are born, but they still have to hit the courts and practice.

It is an honor to have received the gift of teaching, but we still have to develop it. We have to study, practice, learn by trial and error. And, as we hone our teaching skills, we must remember the judgment that James speaks about so that we don't take our calling lightly.

Teaching is not what we do but who we are.

If you sell shoes, you work for a while, then you go home. If you fix cars, you work for a while, then you go home. If you teach, you are a teacher twenty-four hours a day. You may walk away from the classroom, but you can never walk away from your thoughts—images of students will pop into your mind, sometimes at awkward moments when you really should be focusing on something else; ideas for the lesson you are preparing will arrive in a blinding flash; or you may cringe in embarrassment as you recall a time when you didn't have an answer for a student.

People who don't teach can't understand how consuming it is. "What do you mean it's hard? You teach only about an hour every Sunday morning. What could be so time-consuming about that?" We who have experienced the lifestyle called teaching can only shrug our shoulders and walk away feeling rather lonely and wondering about the stress and anxiety that we really can't explain.

How do we tell non-teachers that when we respond to the call to teach, we have decided to go to bed every night for the rest of our lives with the feeling that we haven't finished the day yet? Every night, we lie there collecting our thoughts with that ever-present thought that we might have done something more that day to have made ourselves better teachers.

Just as we will never walk away from our thoughts, we also never walk away from our shadow. Wherever we go, whomever we meet, we cast a shadow as teachers, and people look at us with different expectations. We are to walk like teachers, talk like teachers, act like teachers. We can't suspend the rules, even for a moment. During class, we tell our students how to identify and list the principles of Christlike living. We set up discussion groups and videos and "make it and take it" activities to help drive this knowledge permanently into their being. But to truly show them how the lesson works, we have to demonstrate those principles—not just for an hour a week but twenty-four hours a day. This, too, is part of the judgment.

How we teach what we teach is important.

In 1991, my wife Mary and I traveled to Ukraine to spend a year teaching English at a government university. Living there wasn't easy. We shared a small apartment with a Ukrainian family. We washed our clothes in the bathtub and hung them to dry all around the apartment. We rode trolley buses so crowded that they offered not only transportation but free massages in the process. We ate potatoes—lots of potatoes—and took cold showers.

Teaching wasn't always easy either. In the university where we taught, attendance was a problem. Students were not always eager to learn. Our textbooks were fifty years old, and the blackboards didn't work. But there we met Maria, a twenty-five-year-old college teacher. She was brilliant—maybe one of the most brilliant persons I have ever known. Because Maria was so intelligent and so fluent in

16

English, the American evangelists selected her to translate their messages when they preached to the huge stadium audiences. Maria translated the Word and the exegesis effectively and thousands became believers. But for Maria, it was all just a language drill. She never accepted a word the evangelists said.

One day, my wife Mary came into our office, threw her books down, and exclaimed, "I'm having a bad day. In fact, I'm having a bad week."

Maria protested. "Mary, I don't think you are having a bad week. Yesterday, I went to your English class and as I was watching you teach, I said to myself, 'Oh, that's what a Christian is.'" Because of your example, I've decided that I want to be a Christian too. I am a believer now! I think you are having a very good week."

After that revelation, we spent much time with Maria. We went to Bible studies together. We traveled to the churches in the villages. We even wrote a little book about our time in Ukraine, and Maria wrote about a third of it.

When we returned to the United States, we continued to correspond with Maria. One day, the letters stopped. When we visited Ukraine again, we found her, discouraged and depressed. She had been sick and had had a kidney removed, but she thought she was getting better. We corresponded for a while, but again the letters stopped. Some Americans traveling in Ukraine met Maria and managed to bring her to the United States for treatment, but she had cancer, and it was too far advanced. Maria went back to her homeland; and in the summer of 1996, she died.

Hers is not a sad story. In fact, it is a happy story because our friend Maria is in Heaven. Knowing that is enough to make all our efforts worthwhile—living in cramped quarters, riding crowded buses, taking cold showers, staying up late at night to hand copy materials for class the next day because the blackboard didn't work. One student's eternity is worth all the effort we put into the process.

Every class you and I teach is full of Marias waiting to see how a Christian teaches. It is important for us to remember that it was Mary's method of teaching and not the content of the lesson that moved Maria to seek a relationship with God. That is the stricter judgment we have accepted.

Chapter 2

The Ultimate Teaching Credentials

Galatians 5:22, 23

"But the fruit of the Spirit is love, joy, peace, patience, kindness, goodness, faithfulness, gentleness, and self-control."

Galatians 5:22, 23

"We don't have one single course to help teachers develop the most important quality of teaching."

 What are the credentials of a great teacher? What credentials did our own teachers have? What credentials do we want our children's teachers to have? What credentials should we look for when we advise young people to become teachers? What credentials should a church look for when it chooses people to staff the Sunday schools? Children's church? Youth ministry? Adult training programs? Vacation Bible school?

If we worked at it, we could probably generate a two-page list of credentials we would like to find in anyone teaching. Since that is a rather staggering thought, let me condense all those credentials into four:

- Good teachers care about their students.
- Good teachers are confident.
- Good teachers know the subject matter.
- Good teachers know methodology.

Although some might make adjustments to the list, most of us, including the educational experts, agree that these are the credentials of good teachers; and most of us would agree that the credentials appear in order of importance. We have an abundance of documentation, both anecdotal and statistical, to convince us that the first quality of good teachers is that they care.

During the last twenty years, my fellow teachers and I have committed much effort to the task of impacting the process of teachers' education. My colleagues at the university work hard to make sure that our future teachers have a good handle on subject matter. I work hard to help them develop teaching methods. After these students have successfully completed four years of college training, they still have to take a state-required test to guarantee their proficiency in subject matter and methodology before they can be certified as teachers.

But our list of *four* credentials presents a problem. We have specific courses to prepare teachers in the third and fourth qualities on the list—subject knowledge and teaching methodology—and we test to ensure that all teachers have some measure of ability in these qualities (to give them confidence). But we don't have one single course to help teachers develop and grow in the most important quality of teaching—that of caring—and we have absolutely no way to test to see if the teaching prospect has one iota of caring capability.

A few years ago, the experts in teacher education saw this dilemma, so they created courses in such things as sensitivity training with the purpose of producing caring persons. These experts soon saw the futility of this effort, and most of those courses have now disappeared from the curriculum.

But we still have the problem, both with professional teachers and church volunteers. We know the importance of the quality of caring. We know that teachers with a great capacity to love their students will be effective, even if they may not be as capable as others in subject matter and teaching methodology. We do want teachers who care. We just don't know how to teach that quality, and we have no way to measure who has it and who doesn't.

So now we ask the all-important questions: How do you define care? Where does care come from? For answers, we turn once again to that great educational methods book, the Bible. In his letter to the Galatians, Paul provides us a list of the characteristics of a caring teacher: love, joy, peace, patience, kindness, goodness, faithfulness, gentleness, and self-control. That's it—a good description of the personality of a caring teacher—the kind we want teaching in every class in our program. And where do these qualities come from? They are the fruit of the Holy Spirit. A teacher who continually seeks the guidance of God's Holy Spirit, a teacher who is open to the correction of the Holy Spirit, will be a teacher who embodies these characteristics.

Every educator I know, from the Sunday school superintendent to the most radical, anti-Christian administrator in the public school sector, to the card-carrying Communist still teaching in the former Soviet Union, all agree that these caring qualities are the characteristics most desirable in teachers. Teachers who live out these attributes accomplish more with their classes.

I have a strong urge to pause here and take the list apart and write a comment on each of the nine characteristics, explaining how good teachers show each one, and to give examples of how each one affects the quality and result of teaching. But there is one word in the text which causes me to rethink that urge. Paul tells us that these nine characteristics are the fruit of the Spirit. Notice the singular. These are not fruits of the Spirit; instead they are the fruit of the Spirit. From that word, I conclude that this is a package deal. Those nine characteristics come tied together. We don't write them on a list one by one, hang the list on our wall, and tick them off as we have mastered each. We come to them all at once.

These characteristics in our personality are not the result of our intentional, programmed efforts to develop each. They come to us when we commit ourselves to Jesus Christ so fully that his Spirit fills us to capacity. That is when we have the fruit of the Spirit.

I once watched a powerful speaker with an unforgettable glove illustration. She showed us a glove—limp and shapeless. She then began to slide her hand into it, explaining how her hand represented the Spirit and the glove represented us. As she moved her hand further into the glove, we watched it take shape; but as she pointed out, it still didn't look very complete or very formed until her hand was allowed

25

to fill every nook of each finger. We, too, are shapeless until we are filled completely with the Spirit.

The conclusion is logical: Teachers who are filled with the Spirit are caring teachers. It's that simple.

We go to seminars for teacher training. We read books looking for tips on how to ask questions or how to put together a lesson plan or how to use activities. We analyze our own abilities and gifts. We work at strengthening our weaknesses and utilizing our strengths. And we pray, "God show me how to love, how to be patient."

All of these are good activities which will help us grow, but let's not forget that the first teaching credential we need to address is our personal relationship with our Lord and Savior and our willingness to let the Spirit fill us completely. As we pray, "Lord, help me teach effectively," we first pray, "Lord, fill me with your Spirit."

Chapter 3

See
the Field

Matthew 9:36-38

27

"Ask the Lord of the harvest, therefore, to send out workers into his harvest field."

Matthew 9:38

"There isn't anything wrong with me, Jesus! It's the field that's messed up!"

29

"When he saw the crowds, he had compassion on them, because they were harassed and helpless, like sheep without a shepherd. Then he said to his disciples, 'The harvest is plentiful but the workers are few. Ask the Lord of the harvest, therefore, to send out workers into his harvest field.'"

Matthew 9:36-38

"I don't understand why I have to have both Kevin and A. J. in the same class. I know they are the same age, but I think that we could at least separate them. One of them is bad enough, but when you get the two of them together, they are terrors. How do they expect me to get anything accomplished with both of them at once?"

"I don't spend a lot of time preparing. Only about three people show up every Sunday, anyway."

"The class has grown so large, there just aren't many alternatives. I talk and they listen. That's about all we can do with so many."

"We're just marking time now. When we get the new educational wing built, our Sunday school should really take off."

"Oh well, there isn't anything too urgent in my class. I have the senior women, and most of them have been Christians for fifty years. It isn't as if I am going to say anything new to them."

"I really don't spend much time on Sunday school. I'm just a teaching assistant."

"I don't understand why we can't get better literature. How do they expect us to teach with this?"

"Look at this room—the back room of the basement! What can I get done in these surroundings? Even I'm depressed by this place."

"You know how people are at this age. They're going through that stage where they don't care about learning anything. Well, two can play that game. I'll just bide my time until they grow out if it."

"As you know, I teach in a public school, and there just isn't much opportunity to witness for Christ in that situation!"

Shame on us! Maybe you aren't guilty, but I am, and so are the people I talk with. "There isn't anything wrong with me, Jesus; it's the field that is all messed up. I could be a much more effective worker if I had a better field." How we complain about every little detail.

I can hear Jesus chiding us now. "There isn't anything wrong with the field. The field is ready. Where are the workers?" Now we must learn this lesson.

The first step in assessing the field assigned to us is to recognize Jesus as the Great Arranger. Jesus knows that you have Kevin and A. J. in the same class. Jesus knows that you teach in the back room of the basement. Jesus knows how many come and how many don't. Jesus knows that you are a teaching assistant.

Not only does he know, but he arranged it all with a definite purpose. Jesus gave you your field. He put together the field, and he picked you specifically for it. It is all by design. If we had his infinite wisdom, we might know the purpose for the arrangement, and maybe someday we will know; but for right now, we prepare our lessons, we conduct our classes, and we assess our results with the assurance that Jesus has arranged it.

Frequently I get a glimpse of how Jesus works as the Great Arranger and I respond by standing in awe with my mouth open and saying, "Thank you, Jesus"

As I write this, Mary and I are teaching at a university in central China. When we first decided to come to China for the year, we were assigned to a coastal city in northern China. We researched the place, learned how to pronounce it, made plans, and bought supplies to live and teach in a city on the sea. About three weeks before we were to leave, we were unexpectedly and abruptly reassigned to another university in another city. We were not pleased with the sudden change in plans because we had our hearts set on the other field. We didn't want to come here, and we grumbled, "Why us, Jesus? Why here?"

As soon as we arrived, we saw immediately that this is the perfect spot for us. The teaching opportunities and the personalities of the university officials are exact matches to who we are and what we do best. We have every opportunity to use our approach in the process.

One week after we arrived in the landlocked city, I discovered that I have a rather serious allergy to certain kinds of seafood that are a big part of the diet along the coast. If we had gone to the other place, I would have had to spend the year picking through food and embarrassing myself and our gracious Chinese hosts. The amazing part of this story is that I did not know that I had that allergy until I got here. But Jesus knew about it. He arranged this field for us so that we would have a more productive year. In this same way, Jesus has put you in your specific field. You may not know why yet, but he does.

The second step in assessing our field is for us to see the abundant crop that needs to be harvested. Regardless of our role in the process, regardless of the age or status of our students, there is always a sense of urgency about our work in the field. I have learned about the urgency, not through success but through regrets.

How I would like to have had just five minutes more with David before he took his life; with Kathy before she got pregnant at age fifteen; with Dorothy before she had her heart attack; with Alan before he learned that he had been dismissed in his company's down-sizing. I know that I can't solve their problems. In fact, most of the time I feel helpless and worthless when I see how little I have to offer, but I still sense the urgency when talking to hurting people.

Taking the time and effort to "see the field," is a teaching method. Nothing is more instructive in how to prepare lesson plans, nothing is more helpful in developing materials, nothing is more persuasive in planning learning activities, nothing is more powerful in creating enthusiasm than for us to see our assignment as Jesus saw the fields that day—ready for harvest and crying out for workers. If we want to learn how to be more effective teachers—professional, efficient, creative, innovative, and on the cutting edge in the latest methods and technology—the first seminar we should attend is one where we sit alone with Jesus and look at our field through his compassionate eyes.

Chapter 4

Relationships Before the Lesson

John 4:1-30

"Come, see a man who told me everything I ever did."

John 4:29

"Insecurity rarely looks like insecurity. Almost always, it comes in some other costume."

 Let me guess; you knew that sooner or later I would use the passage where Jesus taught the Samaritan woman at the well. And why not? In all of the methods books ever written, there is no better example of effective teaching than what we find in his encounter with her.

Suppose that Jesus had used a less personal approach. Suppose he had said, "Take a seat, please. We must get started quickly. I still don't understand why you can't come to class when your fellow students do. Get out your notebook and pen and write as I speak. Today's lesson is about the water of life. The outline has three parts: 1) The history of the water; 2) The characteristics of the water; and 3) The substance of the water. Write quickly. There will be a test on Thursday."

"Wait," you protest. "That would never do. That woman was not ready to learn about anything, let alone the water of life. She had not come to hear a lecture. Her mind was not on learning—she brought too much personal baggage with her."

Of course she did, and so do our students. You and I have students in our classes whose personal problems would make this woman's life seem almost normal. Every student we have brings some kind of personal baggage to every class we teach.

Recognizing that fact is the beginning of effective teaching. If our students came to class with their lives and

38

minds free of distractions, eagerly waiting for us to spew out great points of wisdom, teaching would be easy, and anybody could do it. But that isn't reality. There in your class is little Megan whom other children tease because she is overweight. There is the beautiful and talented teenage Laura who lives with the frustration that her parents are pressuring her to achieve even more. There is the young couple who has just learned that their baby has a heart murmur. There is Mrs. Henderson. She needs a new refrigerator and is wondering how she can pay for it out of her Social Security check.

Each student, regardless of age, experiences, or spiritual maturity, slips into your classroom carrying a world of personal baggage on his or her shoulders. For each one, this baggage becomes a barrier between him and your lesson despite his own learning efforts or even your application of the lesson to his needs.

Our first task as effective teachers is to break down that barrier. We accomplish this by establishing a personal relationship with each of our learners. Somehow we have to get beyond language and teaching techniques to discover some bond of trust, something that unites the two of us in the common endeavor of life, something that says to that student, "I am genuinely interested in you as a person. I know you are carrying some baggage, but if you will permit me to enter into your world, I am eager to help you bear some of that burden."

This is what Jesus accomplished with his student at the well. We learn from the text that she came to class with a whole plethora of personal problems. But all of those problems arose from one core issue: She didn't like herself very much. Jesus knew this. She had come to the well when no one else was there. She had purposely avoided the camaraderie that her neighbors enjoyed—the friendly discussion of weather and rising prices, the gossip, the idle chitchat. She knew she was not accepted by them and she didn't want to be seen.

We have students like this woman. We can't always know what past problems have left them with feelings of insecurity, and it isn't always necessary to know the past, but it is important to recognize the many masks that insecurity hides behind. Insecurity rarely looks like insecurity, particularly in children and teenagers. Almost always, it comes in some other costume.

- Sometimes insecurity looks like apathy. "I don't want to play. This is a dumb game."
- Sometimes insecurity looks like arrogance. "I won't waste my time on this."
- Sometimes insecurity looks like boasting. "If I brag on myself, you won't know that I can't do it."
- Sometimes insecurity looks like bullying behavior. "You don't like me, so I may just beat you up."
- With adults, insecurity often looks like absenteeism or even church hopping.

With all these forms of behavior, people are trying to tell us something. "I don't like me—at least not right now; and I'm not quite ready to focus on this lesson."

After forty years of teaching, I have concluded that my students' feelings of insecurity, their lack of self confidence, their feelings of inadequacy, or their low self esteem are the biggest obstacles to my effectiveness as a teacher. If I somehow find a way to penetrate these barriers, I have taken a giant stride toward becoming a better teacher.

Jesus, the Master Teacher, shows us a good technique for tackling the problem. He gave the Samaritan woman a task she could complete. When he asked her for some water, he was acknowledging that he didn't have a way to draw water, and she did. He was also allowing her to get beyond herself for a moment and think of someone else's problem. Jesus was saying to her, "You have something I need. You can be of service to me."

Look how easy that is! How simple and subtle! Great teaching is not some highly complex, deeply philosophical system of theorems and postulates. It is simply understanding human nature, and responding to personal needs. The Master shows us how.

Of course, applying this little tip is not always easy. Sometimes we have to search to discover what it is the student can do, but there is something that every student in my class can contribute to me, the class, or humanity in general. I just need to find out what his ability is and provide him with the opportunity to display it. Recently a youth pastor told me that he has transformed his youth group with one simple dose of this medicine. He turned the meetings over to the teenagers. He helped them get organized but gave them all the responsibility of leading the singing and games, teaching, and providing refreshments. With a little encouragement from the youth pastor and the other adult sponsors, the teenagers took off. Everyone is working. The students say that they are growing. Attendance has doubled.

Are we to assume that a teenager can organize a logical lesson and deliver it as fluently as the youth pastor? Perhaps not, but we may be surprised at the talents that burst forth. And in their efforts, those teens are learning because they have accepted the responsibility for their learning. They are also gaining confidence in themselves because the youth pastor used the principle that Jesus taught us at the well: Give them something they can do.

Recently I attended a homecoming service at a small but growing church. It was to be a big day with special music, a guest speaker, and a covered dish dinner afterward. Before the service started, I was standing in the parking lot discussing the upcoming day with the pastor when a man walked up and announced that he lived right around the corner. He had heard of the church, and had decided to come to check it out. After we had exchanged pleasantries about the weather and the hopes of the local football team, the pastor said to the man, "I have to set up some chairs for a Sunday school class. Would you have a few minutes to come help me?"

As the two walked into the building, I thought, "Poor Pastor. You just made a big mistake. That isn't the way you treat first-time visitors. Everyone knows that you are supposed to give them a big name tag that will make them look conspicuous, and then give them a ball point pen containing the message that Jesus loves them right next to the church phone number. You don't drag them off to help set up chairs."

As the day progressed, I kept noticing the visitor. He sang with enthusiasm. He listened intently to the guest speaker, and at dinner he went back for seconds and maybe thirds. As I was driving out of the parking lot late in the day, I spotted him again. This time he was carrying two bags of trash out to the dumpster in the alley. He waved at me and yelled, "Thanks for coming to visit. Please come again the next time you are in town." How does it happen that in the space of one day, a man moves from first-time visitor to unofficial church greeter? Maybe the pastor was wiser than I thought. Maybe he knew something about the methods of Jesus.

- "I want to teach. I want to tell others why I love history."
- "I want to teach. I want to tell others what I have learned about life."
- "I want to teach. I want to tell others about a Savior who loves us so much that He died for us."

These are all noble purposes but notice the emphasis on "I want to tell. . . ." There comes a time when we need to say, "I want to teach. I want to listen to what others have to say. I want to hear my students tell their stories." As with all good teaching, applying this simple technique requires some planning. Actually learning to listen might require a change in our attitude and in our priorities. But somehow we need to learn how to carry this insight into our classroom regardless of whether we are teaching a group of seven junior high girls or seventy-five young adults. One of the quickest and surest techniques to improve the effectiveness of our teaching is to hold a personal conversation with each student where we can practice that skill of interactive listening.

This technique has many applications Almost every day some teacher asks me about some behavior problem. As an example, take a boy in a junior high class who won't sit still. He is constantly disturbing and interrupting the class. The teacher has tried everything from jovial reprimands to harsh punishment. So far nothing has worked.

I recommended listening. Catch that guy someplace where he least expects you. You could keep him after class, but it would be even more effective to bump into him in the hall after church or on the playground. Be friendly and kind. Say, "Hello, A. J., I'm glad to see you. Gotta minute? I have a problem I want to ask your advice about. I have a student in my class who is really becoming a nuisance—he disturbs the class and interrupts the lesson. I can't teach while he is goofing off, and it's not fair to the other students. What would you recommend that I do? How would you handle that problem?"

Now, just stand back and listen when A. J. talks. He will soon realize that he is the antagonist in the scene, and he just might provide you with very valuable information. In this personal conversation, you have accomplished two goals. You have begun to establish a relationship, and you have encouraged A. J. to assume some of the responsibility of controlling his own behavior.

I know that as teachers we are not supposed to have favorite students and that we are to love them all the same, and we probably do! But the truth is that we do like some better than we like others. We do have favorites and non favorites. Through the years, I have discovered that my non favorites are those I don't know very well. Consequently, the solution to my problem is to get better acquainted with them.

In other words I need to hold a personal conversation during which I spend most of my time listening. I have met students who have discovered this technique themselves, and they aren't afraid to use it. I have seen junior high students cause enough trouble in class to earn a detention so that they can spend some time with their teacher after school in a personal conversation. How effective is that? I have heard teachers say, "I don't know what happened. I didn't like Seth very much at first, but he has become one of my favorites." Oh, the power of listening.

Jesus confronted the woman at the well about the multitude of men in her life (v. 18). Yet he continued to listen as her conversation quickly veered onto the subject of Jewish and Samaritan worship controversies (vv. 19, 20). Sure, her comments were a little off of the topic. But Jesus did not take her to task for giving an irrelevant response or insist that she return to the "husband" issue that he had raised. Rather, he responded to the woman's comments about the proper place to worship (vv. 21-24). This led to the subject of the Messiah. Then, and only then, was Jesus able to teach the main point of his lesson (vv. 25, 26). He got to present his information by allowing the woman to take her own route to get there.

That's why the experts call this technique interactive listening. It encourages the other person to continue to talk. Jesus knew from the beginning of the conversation what needed to be said. But instead of lecturing, he listened. He encouraged the woman. He treated her as a significant person. The lesson was more than a discourse about the water of life. It was an interchange between two people— each sharing their personal character—one, an adulterous woman and the other, the Messiah. Before he started the lesson, Jesus established the relationship.

We know that this lesson was successful. Just look at the results (vv. 39-42)! I find this one to be of the most remarkable stories in the Bible.

The Samaritan woman got up from the lesson, went back into town, marched straight up to the mayor and the town council, and told them what had happened to her. Guess what happened then! They followed her back out to the well. Think about that. An hour or so before, she had not one shred of credibility in that town. No one wanted to be around her. The others ladies surely gossiped about her. She was the object of scorn and ridicule. But after one lesson with Jesus, she had the persuasive ability to get the town leaders to follow her.

I have often wondered what changed so drastically. Did she walk differently? Was there a fresh look on her face? Was it enthusiasm in her voice? What happened to transform that social outcast into a civic leader in only one lesson? I don't know, but I do know the result of successful teaching.

We have a young school bus driver in our town who inherited the route into our poverty-stricken area. Rather than the high-rise government buildings of many cities, our low-income area features house trailers in need of repair, weeds growing everywhere, junk and old car bodies in yards. Life in that part of town is not easy, particularly for the children. Family relationships sound like something from a T.V. talk show. Some children don't live with parents. Some don't have enough to eat. Many have an almost chronic condition of head lice. Most don't have an ample supply of love.

The bus driver became concerned for the seventy-two children who rode his bus, so he established a tutoring program. He borrowed a tent from a funeral home, and he recruited tutors from the student body of the university in town. To lure the children to his weekly Wednesday night session, he fed them pizza after the lessons.

After one year in that tutoring program where university students and children developed relationships, nineteen of those seventy-two children on that bus made the honor roll at their respective schools. That is the success of the relationship-first method of teaching. Maybe Jesus' students didn't have to take the SAT, but his methods still produced results.

Chapter 5

Firm, Fair, and Friendly

1 Peter 3:15, 16

49

"But do this with gentleness and respect."

1 Peter 3:15

"To teach God's Word as if it were simply an alternative lifestyle choice would be a disservice to God—and to your students."

 Forty years ago, my professor of teaching methods came to class one day, adjusted his glasses as if he wanted to establish eye contact with each of us, stood as if to indicate that he would speak with authority, and assumed a tone as if his idea was a special revelation. "When you become teachers," he paused and stared at each student, "remember to be firm, fair, and friendly."

I thought, "The man is a genius! What wisdom! The complete teacher's handbook reduced to three adjectives! And alliterated too!" This was the best I had ever heard.

So I borrowed it. Actually, I stole it. Now that I am a methods teacher, I imitate him. Every semester I do exactly what he did, copying every gesture, every pause, and every vocalization. I don't know whether any of my students have ever said, "The man is a genius," but I must humbly admit that I have the act down rather well. I thought about giving my former professor credit, but after forty years, surely his behavior is in public domain by now.

Not long ago I was reading a methods textbook written during the first decade of this century. Guess what I found? Instructions to teachers to be firm, fair, and friendly! It was not original with my professor. He probably stole it from his professor who stole it from his professor. This has probably been going on for centuries, and I thought I had a monopoly on the idea! Then one day while doing my devotions, I found the source. Although the words aren't exactly the same, the ideas are all there in these two wonderful verses from Peter: "But in your hearts set apart Christ as Lord. Always be prepared to give an answer to everyone who asks you to give the reason for the hope that you have. But do this with gentleness and respect, keeping a clear conscience, so that those who speak maliciously against your good behavior in Christ may be ashamed of their slander."

- "I want to be the kind of Sunday school teacher who makes a lasting impact on my students so that each precious one will find the narrow way which leads to eternity with Jesus."
- "I want to be the kind of professional teacher who communicates to each student the joy of learning and the dignity that God breathed into each one of us as he formed us in his image."
- "I want to be a teacher anywhere I am needed, and I want to be good at it."

What noble commitments—and I hear them every day! But let me whisper to you a secret for your development in becoming the teacher you want to be: *There are no secrets.* Everything that you need to succeed is there in the words of Peter summarized into three alliterated adjectives; be firm, fair, and friendly. Every day a teacher says to me, "The one thing I want my students to know is that I care for them."

That is so important. In fact, it is so important that somebody even put it into a slogan: "They don't care how much you know until they know how much you care." But we cannot communicate a deep level of commitment to our students simply by telling them that we care. We must be willing to share our time, our resources, our lives with them until they know that we are committed to them and they feel secure as learners in our class. Peter tells us how to make the statement.

Good teachers are firm.

"The problem with Christians is that they are so dogmatic," people say to me. If by "dogmatic" they mean that we are certain of our salvation, secure in our knowledge of God's love, and convinced of the truthfulness of God's Word, then of course we are dogmatic. Peter says, "Set apart Christ as Lord." That's pretty dogmatic—doesn't leave much room for alternatives. He continues, "Always be prepared to give an answer to everyone who asks you to give the reason for the hope that you have." If I don't give my students a full account of the reason for my hope, if I do not stand firm in my devotion to God, I have cheated them. God's Word is firm, it is clear. God gave us the Ten Commandments, not the Ten Suggestions. To teach God's Word as if it were simply an alternative lifestyle choice would be a disservice to God—and to your students.

54

There are days when I am not sure about my lesson plans. There are days when I don't know whether my questions will work. There are days when my transparencies are not colorful. There are days when I am not all that confident that I am fully prepared. But every time I walk into that classroom, I carry with me complete hope through my faith in Jesus, my Lord and my Savior. This is what provides me the confidence to teach every lesson.

One way that we demonstrate care for our students is to leave absolutely no doubt in their minds that we have discovered joy unspeakable and peace that passes understanding. So yes, be firm in your faith, and communicate your confidence in God's Word to your students.

Good teachers are fair.

I may tell some jokes and I may use games to get the point across, but the lesson is serious. Standing firm to communicate my hope in Jesus requires that I establish some expectations. Call them what you wish—classroom rules or tyrannical tirades, but fairness demands that I create an atmosphere in which all my students can learn at the maximum of their capacity. If I do not set some expectations or if I do not enforce the expectations, I am not being fair. Before you nod your endorsement of this, let me remind you of how difficult it is to carry out what I have just said. I don't mind making rules. In fact, making rules can be fun. But enforcing the rules fairly is not always enjoyable. I don't want to come across as an ogre. I don't want to make my students angry. They might not come back, particularly if they are adults.

But fairness demands that I do everything I can to create a learning climate. I can't show favorites, and I can't hold grudges. As Peter reminds me, there may be some students "who speak maliciously against your good behavior." Not all of my students are going to sit on the edge of their seats and pledge their burning respect for me and every word I say. Some will disagree. Some will act disinterested. Some will shake their heads in a negative way. Some will work on something else. Some will bother their neighbors. Some will stare at me in disbelief. But, as Peter says, teach "with gentleness and respect." And if you live what you teach, you will answer your critics not with words but by the way you live.

If you have been a teacher for any length of time, you have experienced the wisdom of Peter's point. You have had some students come to you weeks, months, or even years later, and say, "I owe you an apology. I once disagreed with your method or your idea. But now I realize I was wrong and you were right." We need those times of affirmation to give us the answer to stay fair.

Good teachers are friendly.

My heroes are the volunteer teachers in our church programs. These people are the salt of the earth. They work long and hard, faithfully and tirelessly—without pay and often without too much affirmation or encouragement, but the thing that amazes me is what some of them accomplish, particularly in this area of friendliness.

"Build a relationship with your students," we tell professional classroom teachers. "This is vital to your teaching effectiveness and to their growth." So the teachers work on the relationship. Elementary teachers have the students in class about twenty-five hours per week, so they have time to work on the relationship. Secondary teachers have students in class at least five hours a week—still long enough to exchange the data and feelings necessary in a relationship.

Church teachers have students one hour per week, yet many of them still build relationships. They are true artists of this principle of friendliness. Obviously, they are living examples of Peter's instruction to be firm, fair, and friendly with an emphasis on gentleness and respect.

We may stress other aspects of teaching, but I am convinced that nothing has greater impact then the quality of friendliness. If we want to teach effectively, if we want to make a difference, we must show genuine concern for our students. If they perceive that we care, our lessons will find an important spot in their memory banks so that our teaching continues long after the class is over.

Last week I asked 125 college students to write an essay describing their favorite teacher from high school or middle school. Almost forty percent of those students wrote about a teacher who had visited them when they were sick. I am sure all their teachers were good. I am sure they had tons and tons of wisdom to impart. I am sure they stayed up late to plan lessons and grade papers. But five years later, the students remember the time the teacher visited them.

I think that we all need to put that insight into our teaching bank and use it frequently. As teachers, we never get to all the tasks we should; but when we prioritize our tasks so we will have some idea of what we might leave undone, we need to put statements of friendliness, such as visits to a sick student, at the top of the list.

I hear supportive testimony almost every day. Recently a friend told of his experience. He teaches a class of men over fifty-five. (I am always intrigued by the criteria different churches use to construct classes.) About a year ago, a man started visiting almost regularly. Although he mingled well and took part in the class, he showed no inclination that he wanted to join the class or the church. The teacher wondered why, but didn't force the issue. When the teacher heard that the regular visitor was in the hospital, he dropped by for a casual chat. The sick man was deeply moved by the gesture. Although he was not a member, he, too, was worthy of a visit. He was so moved that he promised the teacher that as soon as he was well, he would officially join the church and take an active role in the class .

"Why have you taken so long to reach this step?" the teacher was brave enough to ask.

"I didn't want to give up the visitor spot in the parking lot," the man responded. Again, friendliness made the difference.

Be firm, be fair, be friendly. In two short verses, Peter captures the best wisdom of centuries of pedagogical theory.

Chapter 6

Produce
a **Protégé**

2 Timothy 1:5

"I have been reminded of your sincere faith, which first lived in your grandmother Lois and in your mother Eunice."

2 Timothy 1:5

"Someone is watching us—every gesture, every word."

 Paul wrote to his young protégé, "Timothy, I know that you are a man of faith, but I am not surprised because I know which literature program your church used when you were a boy in Sunday school." Actually, he didn't say that. I just made it up to appease the publishers who produce literature.

Paul wrote to his young protégé, "Timothy, I know that you are a man of faith, but I am not surprised because I have seen your library card. I know that you read books written by the pillars of the faith who can instruct us in the ways of spiritual growth." Actually, he didn't say that either. I just made that up to appease the writers and librarians who contribute to our education.

Paul wrote to his young protégé, "Timothy, I know that you are a man of faith, but I am not surprised because I know who your teachers were in the synagogue." Actually, he didn't say that either. I just made it up because I want to think we teachers have some value in the process.

This is really what Paul wrote, "Timothy, you are a man of faith, but I am not surprised because I know your grandma and your mother." That's the whole crux of excellent education in a nutshell. Regardless of the quality of literature, regardless of the quality of the books we read, regardless of the quality of our overhead transparencies and our lesson plans and our classroom antics, our students learn most of what it is that shapes their characters from watching it lived before them.

That statement is not some astoundingly brilliant insight that I have come to after years of study, observation, and research. We all know it. We see living examples of it every day. Besides that, we know something else stated in Paul's letter to his protégé. We know the valuable role of parents in our lives. We have hundreds of references. Of our five teachers—family, school, media, street (peers), and church—we know that family is the most powerful, the most dominant in shaping us into who we are. One great educator once said, "We learn most at the University of Mother's Knee."

We hear loud and clear the words of God spoken through Moses to the children of Israel that day on the banks of the Jordan River: "These commandments that I give you today are to be upon your hearts. Impress them on your children. Talk about them when you sit at home and when you walk along the road, when you lie down and when you get up" Deuteronomy. 6:7, 8.

We hear Paul's emphatic admonition to the Ephesians: "Fathers, do not exasperate your children; instead, bring them up in the training and instruction of the Lord" (Ephesians 6:4).

To attest to the wisdom of the biblical mandate of the role of the family in our development, we have our own memories—reading while sitting in Daddy's lap, riding the bike with Mom jogging along behind, playing catch with an older brother in the backyard, visiting Grandmother and eating a food we had never eaten before, watching Mother pray, or listening to Dad read the Bible.

A simple but constant reminder of the power of family models is the fact that I grow more like my father every day. The man has been dead for more than thirty years, but he is still teaching me, still influencing my values, my attitude, and even my personality.

These memories bring both laughter and tears. We are indebted to those family members who modeled for our education such virtues as manners, unselfishness, Bible reading, prayer, and worship, and we know that our lives are more complete now because we had the models. However as teachers, we know that some of our students come from homes where these positive family models are at work, but some don't. The question is, what do we do with those students who lack positive models? Surely we don't write them off as doomed to empty lives of failure and heartache, and lives devoid of faith, only because God placed them in a different kind of home situation. The issue of role models and the structure of family life may be one of our most difficult and most crucial challenges as teachers—how to find a way to model the vital lessons for those students who don't have good models at home. I do believe the job can be done. In fact, I believe that the job is being done every week by teachers in churches all across the country. I believe that because I see the results in the college students I meet every day.

Recently, I asked a large number of college students to name the person most influential in their developing their personal value system and world view. Of course, many listed their parents, but many of them named their pastor as the important person in providing value information. This was both shocking and reassuring to me, but what surprised me most was how many of those college students listed their youth pastors as their significant values teacher. From this informal research, I concluded that teaching by modeling is being done effectively in the lives of many of our students. Some have parent models, but others have found very effective models from other sources.

Whether our teaching by modeling takes place in the family or the classroom, we need to remind ourselves constantly of the power and significance of this teaching method, not just for the test on Tuesday but for a lifetime. Like Timothy, we are in part the products of the models we have had, and our students will also live out the values taught by their models. Recognizing the significance of this exciting yet frightening challenge, we need to remind ourselves of some principles that relate directly to the method of teaching by modeling.

We need to remember that we are models.

Someone is watching us—every gesture, every word. They are watching our habits, our moods, our expressions, our integrity, our morality, and our spirituality. It is an awesome responsibility to think that any slip-up on our part could damage someone else. Every time we step into our classroom, we need to hear those silent pleas from hungry learners: "Please help me. Show me how to live effectively. Show me how to apply the Bible to my life. Show me where to find joy unspeakable and peace that passes understanding."

Every so often I have to pause and ask myself, "Will I be pleased if my students imitate my habits? Will I be pleased if they approach Bible reading as I do? Will I be pleased if they begin their prayer life where I begin mine? Will I be pleased if they approach business relationships as I do? Will I be pleased if they set the same standards for entertainment as I have? "These are the haunting questions that accompany the role of being a model.

A few years ago, I had a student who loved the poetry of Carl Sandburg. She was more than a fan; she was passionate about his poetry. A couple of weeks into her student teaching, I went out to watch her instruct a class of high school seniors. I found a seat near the back surrounded by all the other back-row crowd—those trying to get as far away from knowledge as they can. When the class reached that point where I dared communicate with my neighbors, I whispered to the girl on my right, "Who is your favorite poet?"

"Carl Sandburg," she whispered back without hesitation.

I tried it again. "Who is your favorite poet?" I whispered to the boy on my left.

"Carl Sandburg," he whispered back, not ashamed to admit that he had a favorite poet.

I tried it once more. "Who is your favorite poet?" I whispered to the girl in front.

"Carl Sandburg," was her quiet reply.

More coincidence? I don't think so! But the fact that this student teacher's enthusiasm for Carl Sandburg was adopted by many of her students is a convincing reminder that the lessons we model can have a significant impact on the choices our students make, even when we wonder whether they are paying attention to us.

Lessons taught by modeling have a long future.

Although we may not see any noticeable immediate response, although we may not see any drastic increase in the kind of knowledge that can be measured on a test, we need to remember that we are teaching nonetheless. Someday, long after they have forgotten what literature we used and what material we studied, maybe even after they have forgotten our names and what we looked like, they may still be opening their prayers as we did; reading from the same Bible translation as we did; or greeting their classes as we greeted ours. One of the joys of teaching through modeling is that we have to trust God for the future.

Teaching through modeling is appropriate for all ages.

My mother has an old dog who has lived with her for many years. About a year ago, the dog started a new routine. Mom puts his biscuits in a dish in the kitchen, but the dog, apparently in need of family security, has learned to run into the kitchen, grab a mouthful of biscuits, run back to the living room and lie at mom's feet while he eats his dinner. Who says you can't teach an old dog new tricks? Regardless of the age of your students, you still have people who are looking at you to demonstrate for them how faith works—just as Lois and Eunice did for Timothy.

Chapter 7

Determination
and Persistence

Jeremiah 36

"Take another scroll and write on it all the words that were on the first scroll."

Jeremiah 36:28

"I want to cast my ballot for Baruch for entry into the Teachers' Hall of Fame."

73

There is no question about the lesson to be learned from Jeremiah's example. There is no need to look for hidden meanings or inferences or implications. Jeremiah 36 is a study of determination and persistence in teaching.

Jeremiah, the school principal, was determined to get the lesson to the people—never mind the setbacks, such as not being allowed into the classroom and the king burning your only textbook. The lesson was too important, too vital, too crucial to the whole community. It had to be taught. Fortunately, the principal found a teacher just as determined as he was, and education happened. That's the way education always happens. Determined people teach persistently!

Of course, we know about Jeremiah's place in the history of the church, but I want to cast my ballot for Baruch for entry into the Teacher's Hall of Fame. Can't you just see him sitting there patiently writing down Jeremiah's words— word by word, sentence by sentence, and paragraph by paragraph? And then going to the temple day in and day out to read—reading to anyone who came in, reading and reading without any thought of his own personal comfort, or even safety? Not doing it just once, but starting all over again after the king burned the original scroll! That's persistence, and persistence is an excellent method in education.

In Jeremiah's day and in the twenty-first century, there isn't anything complicated about that kind of commitment. We don't need to study the research or master the latest technology to develop a new vocabulary. To make this point clear, I will put my commentary into the form of some stories of persistent teachers I have known. Because I am the one with the keyboard, I will tell my stories, but while I am in the middle of my story, feel free to remember a teacher who made a difference in your life on the sheer strength of persistence. As we tell our stories, we should both be renewed and inspired by the profound lesson on instructional strategies.

I write this on a bright fall Saturday in central China where we are living for a year. This morning I walked over to a nearby stadium for my daily jog. There on the track was a scene I will never forget: a father and his twelve-year-old daughter with a new bike. You know the rest of the story. You have seen it played out yourself. Timidly, she pedaled, teetering and rocking and swaying as Father ran along with his supporting hands. She would tumble. He would encourage her, and they would start again. Time after time! I wondered how long Father's patience would last and how many skinned knees and elbows she could endure. But they persisted. Finally, that memorable moment came! He turned loose; she was riding by herself. After several other attempts and several trials and errors, she eventually made it all around the track, and while Daughter was cycling around that 400 meters, Daddy stood in the middle of the field and gleefully sang a song.

Of course, it was all in Chinese, and I didn't understand a word, but the lesson is universal, cutting across all languages and cultures. Persistence is effective teaching.

When I was a boy attending a small rural church, Mrs. Henderson was our most faithful member. I have no idea how old she was, but in my boyhood eyes, she was ancient. She had white hair in a tight bun, full skirts, and glasses. She walked with a cane, and her voice quivered when she spoke. Surely, she was too old to be a Sunday school teacher, but she still taught every Sunday. She never missed a Sunday. The oldest and probably most infirm member of our church never missed a Sunday. So what did this epitome of antiquity teach? She surely taught other people her age. No! Mrs. Henderson taught the toddlers. The scene is unforgettable. That old woman sitting in a chair in the middle of the room—children hanging all over and hanging on every word as she told her stories. Creatively, she had made an apron out of flannel, so she could stick the flannel graph characters all over her clothes as she brought to life such people as David and Goliath for hundreds of children over the years.

I still bump into some of those children even now. I don't know what they all do, but those I meet are missionaries, ministers, college presidents, church music directors, worship leaders, educational directors, and even Sunday school teachers. Persistent teaching apparently reproduces itself.

I have a friend who taught high school biology in the same room of the same building for thirty-three years. The only flaw on his record was that he wasn't always dependable. During those thirty-three years, he missed a half day. Think of that: one half day in thirty-three years! Every time I meet a person who had ever been a student in that school, I always ask who their favorite teacher was; and once again I get the story of Mr. Barker who missed a half a day in thirty-three years. After he retired from that same room in that same building, he and his wife moved to Taiwan to teach even more. Persistence is a way of life.

Several years ago, one of my former students took a job teaching in inner-city Chicago. This particular high school was noted for being bad—violent, disruptive students, low test scores. The young teacher encouraged me to come visit him. I didn't want to go, but he was so enthusiastic that I decided I had no choice.

I borrowed a car from the university because I didn't want to drive my own vehicle into that neighborhood, and I went to spend an afternoon. As soon as I drove into the parking lot, I was convinced that I had made a bad decision. I am usually rather secure around adolescents, but not this day. I was frightened. The building was in bad repair with broken windows and graffiti-covered walls and doors. Students were loitering on the lawn and in the doorway and in the halls. I stopped at the office to get directions only to find that I had to travel to the end of the hall and up to the third floor. Timidly, I made my way through the mess. As I peered into the classrooms, I saw chaos. Students were milling around; teachers were busy trying to keep order—not able to do much teaching and so there was very little indication of learning. Then I came to the last room on the third floor—and entered an oasis. Thirty-five students were sitting in an orderly fashion, all listening to a young teacher explain the finer points of grammar. I was more than impressed; I was dumbfounded. In the midst of the most chaotic school I had ever seen, one teacher was having class, orderly and productively.

At the end of the day, we walked together back to my car. This was a large school, more than four thousand students, and I think every one of them was hanging out in the hall that afternoon. The school had a rule forbidding wearing of hats in the building, but in open defiance, almost every student had some kind of hat or cap on. As the students saw us coming, amazingly the hats came off and went behind their backs. "Good evening, Mr. Moore," they all said respectfully as the young teacher passed them. Four thousand students in the building and they all knew this first-year teacher.

Without even trying to hide my disbelief, I asked, "How did you accomplish this?"

He grinned and replied simply, "Persistence."

I learned something that day. Persistent teaching involves more than just longevity. We talk of improving educational programs. We talk of reforming our schools. We talk of reformulating our classes at the church, getting new curriculum, upgrading the technology, but the first step in solving whatever educational problems we may have in our particular situation is to have the kind of teachers that students are willing to take their hats off for! This respect is the result of determination and persistence. Baruch taught us this method in Jeremiah 36.

Chapter 8

Patience and the Aha! Moment

John 14:1-6 - John 20:24-31

"Lord, we don't know where you are going, so how can we know the way?"

John 14:5

"We watch the light come on, the joy radiate in the face, the change in the whole person."

 Jesus had a good lesson that day. No! Jesus had a great lesson. A lesson not just about life but about eternity, full of hope, joy, promise—a lesson powerful enough to pull us through the bumps and bruises of life because we know the reality of God's own Son. What a great lesson!

"Do not let your hearts be troubled. Trust in God; trust also in me. In my father's house are many rooms; if it were not so, I would have told you. I am going there to prepare a place for you. And if I go and prepare a place for you, I will come back and take you to be with me that you also may be where I am. You know the way to the place where I am going."

John 14:1-4

But have you ever noticed that right in the middle of your lesson, no matter how good it is, some student holds up a hand and says something totally irrelevant like, "Does your neck always turn red when you get excited?"

This time it was Thomas, Thomas the concrete thinker, the one who had to see the physical evidence, the empiricist. On that day, Thomas just wasn't ready to comprehend a reality as majestic and wonderful as resurrection and ascension. "I don't get it," he interrupted

Jesus. "I don't know where you're going. How can I know the way?"

Jesus, the Master Teacher, responded with a direct pointed answer which is also profoundly filled with hope and promise, "I am the way, the truth and the life."

What we learn later is that Thomas didn't get that either. Think of it: Thomas spent three years of his life with the greatest teacher who has ever lived. Thomas traveled with him, ate with him, listened to his teaching, assisted in his miracles. And he still didn't get it! That fact in itself ought to provide a bit of encouragement for those of us who struggle in the teaching pit day after day and week after week. Even Jesus had a student who didn't get it.

So what did Jesus do because of his slow learner? He panicked, of course. Frustrated, he cried himself to sleep several nights in a row. He stayed up late to find extra material and to spruce up his overhead transparencies. He even went so far as to write out his resignation and threaten to give it to the superintendent.

No, he didn't. I just made that up because that is what I might have been tempted to do. I want my students to love every lesson, to hang on every word, to mine every nugget, to walk out of every class nodding their heads in approval, knowing full well that their lives have been eternally changed through the experience of the last hour. I can't bear to think that even one of them didn't get it. But Jesus isn't Cliff. He didn't panic. He waited. That is how he responded to this serious setback of his teaching. He waited. Although the lesson that Thomas didn't get was absolutely essential to his life and eternity, Jesus still demonstrated the excellent teaching method of patience. He waited for Thomas to mature and for the next opportunity to reteach the lesson. I suspect that during the wait, Thomas' mind wasn't entirely idle. He had heard the words. He could recite the facts. He just didn't comprehend the depth of the concept.

"Now Thomas (called Didymus), one of the Twelve, was not with the disciples when Jesus came. So the other disciples told him, 'We have seen the Lord!'

"But he said to them, 'Unless I see the nail marks in his hands and put my finger where the nails were, and put my hand into his side, I will not believe it.'"

John 20:24, 25

When the time of the test came, it didn't help much that Thomas's classmates came to report that they had finally mastered the point. They had witnessed the next installment of the lesson. They had, with their own eyes, seen the great "I Am," alive and walking. They now understood what Jesus meant that day of his excellent lesson.

"Not me," Thomas was honest enough to admit. "I still don't get it. Dead is dead. That is what my logical mind tells me. How can I possibly know anything else?"

"A week later his disciples were in the house again, and Thomas was with them. Though the doors were locked, Jesus came and stood among them and said, 'Peace be with you!' Then he said to Thomas, 'Put your finger here; see my hands. Reach out your hand and put it into my side. Stop doubting and believe.'

"Thomas said to him, 'My Lord and my God!'

"Then Jesus told him, 'Because you have seen me, you have believed; blessed are those who have not seen and yet have believed.'

"Jesus did many other miraculous signs in the presence of his disciples, which are not recorded in this book. But these are written that you may believe that Jesus is the Christ, the Son of God, and that by believing you may have life in his name."

John 20:26-31

The day arrived when Thomas stood face-to-face with the living answer to his questions. At that point, all the facts which he had surely pondered through the past few months fell into place, and all he could say was the awed,

"My Lord and my God." Jesus' method of patience bore its fruit.

Some experts tell us that we learn in a gradual continuous progression which they can diagram in what they call the "learning curve."

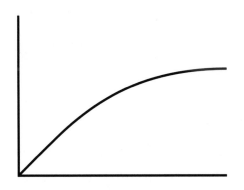

This is a good insight that can help us understand the process our students go through when learning to recite the books of the Bible in order or mastering the memory verses. But I want to propose another type of learning which I will call "aha" learning. There are times when our learning doesn't move forward in a gradual, continuous progression. We put in the effort. We store the facts in our brain. We repeat, we recite, but all through that process, we aren't learning very much. Then one day we have an experience, often at an unexplained rare moment of insight when suddenly we see clearly, and all we can do is exclaim, "Aha, now I know."

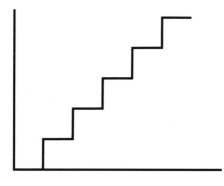

Those "aha" moments are significant in our development. It is the moment when we realize that Daddy turned the bicycle loose, and we are really riding all by ourselves. It is the moment when we realize that the foreign language we have been struggling with for weeks is not just a bunch of grammar rules in a textbook, but it is the way real people communicate with each other. It is the moment when we realize the full impact of our memory verse, "For God so loved the world, that he gave his only begotten Son, that whosoever believeth in him should not perish, but have everlasting life" (John 3:16, *KJV*), and we put our belief in the truth. It is the moment when we, like Thomas, stand face-to-face with the resurrected Savior and exclaim, "My Lord and my God."

How wonderful the enterprise of teaching would be if those "aha" moments came to each of our students every class period! But they don't! Day by day and week by week, we struggle through practicing those techniques we know are effective. We wait, and we develop the method of patience. Then one day without any warning, it happens. One student gets it. We watch the light come on, the joy radiate in the face, the change in the whole person. At that point, we have an "aha" moment in teaching. We say, "This is it. This is why I teach." With renewed enthusiasm, we go back to the grind waiting patiently for the next "aha" moment.

If we could understand the reason why those moments come precisely when they do in our lives, we would surely become wise, famous, and rich. Perhaps it has something to do with background experience. Perhaps it has something to do with the way the connector in our brain works. Perhaps it has something to do with divine instruction. We don't know why they come. They just do.

I can identify with a chemistry teacher who described his own experience. "I explained the concept to the class, but I could see in their faces that they didn't get it. So I explained it again, but I could see in their faces that they still didn't get it. I explained it one more time; and all of a sudden, I got it."

In 1955, when I was an eighteen-year-old college freshmen, I took Old Testament Survey from a great professor, Dr. Rowena Strickland. One day she introduced a passage new to me. Joseph was in Egypt when his brothers came for food. During their conversation, the brothers told Joseph of their younger brother Benjamin who was at home, and Joseph told them they would have to bring him the next time they came. When the brothers gave the news to Papa, Papa did not want Benjamin to go. But brother Reuben made a deal with Papa. "Let Benjamin go with us. If we don't bring him back, you can kill my two sons."

I still remember Dr. Strickland's expression as she worked to get overgrown teenagers to see the depth and the beauty and the richness of that offer. Animated and eloquent she stayed on the point for several minutes. With me, she failed. I didn't get it. I didn't see any beauty in that offer. I saw only a selfish person, out to save his own hide.

About five years ago, I was driving through Kentucky letting my mind fill and wander. For some reason, I went back in memory to college days, and for some reason, I recalled the incident from Old Testament Survey. Remembering from my adolescent perspective, I was about to chuckle, amused by Dr. Strickland's teaching futility. Suddenly I realized I wasn't an overgrown teenager anymore. I was a father and a grandfather. From the perspective of knowing that most parents would die to spare the lives of their children, I suddenly said, "Aha, I get it! Reuben could have offered his own life, but that was his second best. The one thing he had more precious than his own life was the lives of his sons. His promise to bring Benjamin home safely was felt so profoundly that he staked the lives of his two sons on it!

In 1955, Dr. Strickland taught me the facts, the words, but I wasn't ready to comprehend the lesson yet. I needed more experience and more insight from the Master Teacher. What a debt I owe to a teacher who taught well but who had also mastered the method of patience.

One of my own greatest teaching opportunities came not in a classroom but in a courtroom. A few years ago, an attorney called me. He had heard my name somewhere, and he was looking for an expert witness for a trial. Because I had never been to court before and because the trial was fifty miles away (the distance required to make one an expert), I eagerly accepted. When I arrived, I learned something of the case. In an earlier divorce suit, a mother had won custody of two small children. After the divorce, she became a Christian and went to Central America as a missionary, taking the children with her. Father was upset because his children were being educated in a foreign country. I was called to interpret the test scores that indicated that the children were making normal progress.

The whole situation was strange to me, and I am sure I handled it awkwardly. The judge's face testified that he had not smiled for years. A very tense person stood in front of me and made me swear to tell the truth. An epitome-of-efficiency sat with fingers ready to type down every sound that came from my mouth. Under these conditions, I did the best I could. In simple language, I testified that as far as I could tell, both children were average students capable of doing their schoolwork.

When I finished my explanation, the judge leaned over, frowned even more harshly, and said, "I have a question for the expert."

"Yessssss, Sssir?" I answered.

"Do missionaries' children become missionaries?" he wanted to know.

I thought about it, and I answered truthfully. "I don't know. Do lawyers' children become lawyers?"

All of a sudden the judge changed into a person. He smiled and gleefully started telling his story of how his daughters all want to go to law school, but his son isn't all that interested. Dutifully, the epitome-of-efficiency typed it all into the record.

At that point, I gained enough confidence that I decided I could handle this situation. After we had listened to the judge's account of his family tree, he asked if there were other questions of this witness. The father's attorney spoke up. "Yes, I have a question. I want the witness to tell the court what it means to be born again."

So there I sat. I had sworn to tell the truth. The epitome-of-efficiency was sitting with fingers arched. The proud-father judge was bent over the desk staring at me.

I am usually rather glib in explaining what it means to be born again, but in different circumstances. We need to sing "Amazing Grace" first, welcome the visitors, and take up an offering. In a court of law how do you teach nonbelievers what it means to be born again? What words do we use to describe the majesty, the beauty, the power, the freedom, the intensity of God's love? How do we teach the transformed life? In that situation, as in all teaching situations, we do the best we can, pray for the Holy Spirit to bless our humble effort and practice the method of patience. I have absolutely no idea how my little sermon delivered from the witness box affected the lives of those present, but at least I had the opportunity to teach the lesson. All I can do now is practice the method of patience.

Chapter 9

Beyond "See Spot Run"

Acts 8:26-40

"Do you understand what you are reading?"

Acts 8:30

"We don't teach the Bible in Sunday school or church. The book is too big."

 It's called a primer. Sure, it's not classic literature, but without *The Adventures of Dick and Jane,* most of us would never be able to tackle *Moby Dick.* From the innocuous beginnings of "See Spot. See Spot run," we eventually find our way to "Call me Ishmael."

No step is more vital in creating lifelong learners than creating confident readers. When a student is able to pick up a book, read it, and understand it, learning breaks out of the confines of the classroom and into the limitless laboratory of life. I am convinced that God was making that point when he introduced Philip to the eunuch from Ethiopia.

"Now an angel of the Lord said to Philip, 'Go south to the road—the desert road—that goes down from Jerusalem to Gaza.' So he started out, and on his way he met an Ethiopian eunich, an important official in charge of all the treasury of Candace, queen of the Ethiopians. This man had gone to Jerusalem to worship, and on his way home was sitting in his chariot reading the book of Isaiah the prophet. The Spirit told Philip, 'Go to that chariot and stay near it.'

"Then Philip ran up to the chariot and heard the man reading Isaiah the prophet. 'Do you understand what you are reading?' Philip asked.

"'How can I,' he said, 'unless someone explains it to me?' So he invited Philip to come up and sit with him."

Acts 8:26-31

This is one of my favorite Bible stories; it is also one of my favorite stories in the methods book. As a teacher, I find both inspiration and information in this account. First, there is the inspiration of the reality that Philip was in the right place at the right time. As we learn from an earlier text, his meeting the chariot was not a simple coincidence; it was the result of an act of obedience. Sometime earlier, we suspect a few days, we find Philip in the midst of what was apparently a very successful revival in Samaria. Now think of that—an evangelist in the middle of a successful revival! But an angel came and instructed him to go sit by the side of the road. I wonder if Philip might have prayed, "God, are you sure about this? We're having a revival here. People are coming to the knowledge of the Kingdom and are seeing your power. Have I heard right? You want me to leave all this and go sit by the side of the road? Is that the most effective use of my ministry right now?"

Whatever he thought about the assignment, Philip obeyed. There is a lesson for teachers in that response. The assignment with the greatest potential and the assignment that will make the fullest use of our ministry talents is the one we have right now. "Wonderful," we say. "I spent four years of my life preparing to be a teacher and I draw bathroom duties. What a great opportunity!" But if bathroom duty is the opportunity we have, it deserves our best. If we teach an adult class of 1,000, that assignment deserves our best. If we're an aide in a junior boys class, that assignment deserves our best. If we spend too much time complaining about the assignment, we might miss the opportunity.

Philip obeyed the angel and found himself in the right place at the right time. He had come to the roadside to teach one man how to read the Bible. What a noble purpose for a teacher! Reading is a solid foundation for all of learning. Regardless of who our students are, regardless of the content of the lesson, regardless of our own teaching abilities, our first purpose is to teach our students how to read.

Let me make that point emphatically. There is a significant difference in our approach when our purpose is to teach a student how to *read* the material rather than how to learn the material. For many years of my career, I taught literature. I covered the field—poetry, essays, short stories, novels. I introduced students to various authors. I explained tones, themes, and plots. I tried to show my love for the field. But I was discouraged. Somehow I just knew that the students weren't nearly as excited as I was when we had finished the lesson. No matter how fast I talked, I could never cover all the great selections that deserve to be read, and I suspected that the students didn't read much after the term was over. In fact, probably no more than five percent of my students ever read a poem that they didn't have to read for class.

In desperation, I changed my career. I quit teaching literature and started teaching students how to read literature. The changes in my practices might have been subtle, but they were significant. Rather than trying to cover all the material, I chose selected examples. I spent more time helping the students see the value of literature in their lives. I let them explain to me what they got from the reading. In other words, I became a much more effective teacher.

Now, we need to relate this to Bible teaching. In other books I have written and at times when I have addressed fellow-educators, I have made a statement that on the surface seems controversial. Nevertheless, I am convinced that it is a biblical point and is crucial for a successful program of Christian education. Therefore, I will repeat the statement at this time: *"We don't teach the Bible in Sunday school or church. The book is too big."*

My point is not at heretical as it may sound. The fact is, regardless of how fast we talk, regardless of how many seminars we attend, regardless of how many films we show, we won't be able to teach every book, every chapter, every verse, and every word of Scripture. During Sunday school and church time, we can teach only bits and pieces of the Bible. If our students are ever going to learn it all, they will have to read it on their own. Thus, our purpose is to teach people how to read the Bible. We can teach background, such as historical or cultural information, which contributes to understanding. We can teach study techniques, such as using the concordance or language analysis. We can teach the method of life applications. We can communicate our own personal awe for the Word and its relevance and meaning to our lives. Through this, we help our students develop the tools for reading the Bible and applying its wisdom to their own personal pilgrimage. This is why people go to Sunday school—to learn how to read the Bible.

If I have done a good job of developing this point, you should be saying about now, "Well, this is obvious; why don't more of us teachers have this as our primary focus?" Because most of us, unfortunately, don't think about it. Most of us just assume that our students come to class with their Bible-reading skills already in place, and that is one of the most dangerous assumptions teachers can make.

Let's consider Philip's situation. Of all the people coming down the road that day, which one would you assume to be the least likely candidate for some Bible-reading help? On first appearance, that Ethiopian seemed to have it together. He apparently had some money because he was riding in a nice vehicle. He had a good job—high up in the civil service. He was a religious man eager to worship. He was already reading the Bible. Wouldn't logic lead us to the assumption that he could manage on his own? He didn't seem to need much help. If I were the teacher in this situation, I would probably think I should spend my time with some of the other students with more apparent needs. But this was the very person that Philip was sent on the special mission to teach. The conversation between those two men should be indelibly burned into the minds of every one of us who would ever presume to take on the role of teacher. "Do you understand what you are reading?" Philip asked simply and sincerely.

In the response, we hear the sad plea, the cry that represents so many of our students. "How can I unless someone explains it to me?"

Expand the Ethopian's answer: "I don't have a teacher. Please help me. I want to understand. I want to know. I want to see clearly enough to believe, to base my life on the wisdom of the Book. Please teach me to read it. Explain it to me. Tell me what the words mean. Tell me who the people are. Bring it to life for me." How sad the story would have been if Philip had assumed that the Ethiopian could read the Bible on his own! How sad it is when we assume that our students can read! In fact the biggest mistake teachers make is to assume that everyone reads as well as we do.

Recall your own student days and you will remember the frustration with that assumption. Your teacher said, "The homework for tomorrow is to read the next chapter in the book. It isn't long. I read it in twenty minutes last night." At this point, you said to yourself, "Yeah sure! That means I'm in for an hour and a half at least, and then I still won't know enough to pass the quiz." That bitter memory should carry a strong warning for us all. *Our students don't read as well as we do.* They need our help. This is true not only of our students, but also of some people who would really like to be our students but don't come because they are ashamed of their reading ability.

I am going to venture to say that if you live in a typical neighborhood in America, there is someone near you who doesn't attend church, who never hears the Word preached, and who doesn't fellowship with believers simply because that person doesn't read well. Let me ask you a question with an obvious answer, "Can a person who cannot read be a Christian?"

"Of course," you yell at me, impatient with such a stupid question. Now, go to church Sunday morning and imagine that you are a non-reader. Make note of how often you are left out—reading the announcements and order of worship, singing hymns, turning to the Bible text, filling out the visitor's card. There is an obvious conclusion to all of this: church is not friendly to non-readers. I am convinced that the non-reading adults in our communities constitute one of the most overlooked mission fields of the world.

But let's return to those people in our class who need our help in learning to read the Bible. Again, we need to be warned about making assumptions. Some are excellent students. Some are experienced readers. Some are highly educated. Some may have Ph.D.'s in physics. But we need to hear the plea of that highly educated and eager Ethiopian, "I need a teacher to help me read this Book!"

The Bible doesn't read like a physics book, a psychology book, or a philosophy book. There is a special way to approach the Word of God, and that is what our students need to learn. That is the purpose of our teaching. That was Philip's mission. Now we come to the question of how we go about accomplishing this purpose. What is the best technique for teaching reading?

The educational journals are filled with a whole myriad of answers focusing on theories, techniques, methods, procedures—materials of every sort. There is always a body of research to support the claim that not only is one particular technique the *best* for teaching people to read, it just might be the only effective technique. Thus we have books advocating the phonics technique, the traditional technique, the progressive technique, the whole-language technique, etc.

In the midst of all of this, I recommend that we take a long look at the Philip technique. For want of a better name, I call it the "technique of proximity." With instructions from the Spirit, Philip got near his student. He went right up to the chariot to ask his initial question, and then he got into it. He crossed over the learning barrier of physical distance. He got close enough to listen to the man read, and to ask pertinent questions about comprehension level.

Through the years, I have had the opportunity to watch many of the theories about teaching reading put into practice in the classroom. I have studied the various tests and quizzes designed to measure a person's reading ability and to pinpoint the exact accomplishments or weaknesses that person might have. I am sure all these approaches have merit, but through experience I have come to believe that no technique of assessing reading ability is any more reliable or effective than the Philip technique. We simply get close enough to hear the person read, to ask questions, and give help.

I think we already know that. Despite our good teachers in primary school and despite all the classroom activities we participated in, most of us learned to read sitting on a parent's lap close enough to smell Mother's perfume and to feel Daddy's whiskers. That's what I call teaching reading by the technique of proximity.

Of course, we have to find some creative way to apply that technique, particularly if we have thirty fourth graders in junior church, some of whom have learned to read sitting on a parent's lap and some of whom haven't. It is a big challenge, but I am convinced the consequences merit our efforts. I have seen the joy of success, and I have seen the perils of failure.

In 1991, I met Helen while I was teaching at a university in Ukraine. As a twenty-one-year-old student, Helen spoke English almost as fluently as a native American. Not only was she very bright, but she studied English passionately. A couple of years before I met her, Helen saw a poster advertising an American lecture. Hungry for anything English, she went. The lecturer was a well-known evangelist who opened a whole new world for this young student who grew up in a country with a seventy-year history of atheism. He told her about God, and she believed him. He told her that she had a soul and an eternal future, and she believed him. He told her that she needed to study about spiritual things, and she believed him.

When the lecture was over, someone handed Helen a Bible. She rushed home to open her book to discover more about this new world just opened to her. Being a good student and a good reader, Helen knew how to approach a book. She started on page one reading through page by page putting emphasis and thought on every word and every sentence. When she got to the "begat" section, she bogged down in the detail. There was more here than she could decode. She decided she needed a teacher, so she put the Bible aside until she could find help.

One day while she was walking down a street in Kiev, she spotted a young American. She knew he was American because he was smiling (which Ukrainians did not do in public), and because he was wearing American shoes. Boldly, Helen, in desperate need of a Bible teacher, went to the young man and asked him to help her read her Bible. He agreed, of course, because this was the reason he had come to Ukraine—to teach university students how to read the Bible.

He taught Helen. He taught her thoroughly and he taught her effectively. Because of his teaching, when I met Helen two years later, she was one of the best informed and most dedicated cult member I have ever met.

Do you want a story with a happier ending? So do I. In fact, this story serves as a reminder to me every day that regardless of where I am or what I am doing, my first purpose is to teach people how to read the Word. Philip went down to the side of the road to help one man; and that event had mighty significance in the history of the kingdom of God.

Chapter 10

Hand Them a Strainer

Acts 17:10-12

"The Bereans . . . examined the Scriptures every day to see if what Paul said was true."

Acts 17:11

"The good stuff goes through, and the bad stuff is strained off and thrown away."

"As soon as it was night, the brothers sent Paul and Silas away to Berea. On arriving there, they went to the Jewish synagogue. Now the Bereans were of more noble character than the Thessalonians, for they received the message with great eagerness and examined the Scriptures every day to see if what Paul said was true. Many of the Jews believed, as did also a number of prominent Greek women and many Greek men."

Acts 17:10-12

The news was good—Paul was coming to town! The most famous evangelist in the world was going to pay a visit. This man has been commissioned by the finest church in the association. He had suffered persecution and had been mistaken for a deity. He had preached to thousands. He had started churches and established ministries. He had written theology books. He was the director of the Foreign Mission Society. And he was coming to town!

So how did those Bereans respond to all this hype and ceremony? They got out their Bibles just to make sure that Brother Paul was telling it straight. I like those Bereans, and the lesson they teach us is one of the most essential we or our students will ever learn. They teach us the method of "the strainer."

Don't exhaust yourself searching for the profound theological meaning of the term "strainer." In the language of country folks, it's what we pour the milk through. The good stuff goes through while the bad stuff is strained off and thrown away. We need to develop such a strainer for our minds and our lives. Every day we hear ideas. We turn on our T.V. and we get ideas. We read a book and we get ideas. We listen to a speaker and we get ideas. We talk to our friends and we get ideas. Some ideas are good. We need to let them come through, let them soak in, let them become a part of us, move us, and change us.

Some ideas are bad. If we let them come in, they will hurt us, corrupt us, lead us down the wrong path. We need to strain them off and throw them away. To do this, we have to develop a strainer.

Of all the lessons we teach about how to live effective Christian lives, none is more crucial than mastering the ability to strain ideas—processing the good ones and throwing out the bad ones.

To demonstrate this activity, let's test your strainer. Let me present you with three ideas to see how you handle information.

One. When we pull the plug on the bathtub, the water goes gushing out in a clockwise pattern; but in the city of Sao Paulo, Brazil, there is a law which requires the water to gush out of the bathtub in a counter-clockwise pattern.

113

Two. If a cow should bite you with her upper teeth, she would poison you; and you would probably die.

Three. Once, a virgin gave birth.

So let's analyze how your strainer operated on the first two of these statements:

One. Your experience tells you that water does swirl in a clockwise direction when going down a drain. Your experience may tell you further that this happens every time, independent of any effort you make to change it. Your common sense concludes that it is ludicrous to believe that any type of legal pressure would cause natural forces to be reversed.

Nevertheless, you may have some additional material in your strainer. Perhaps you have some travel experience that has taken you into the earth's southern hemisphere. There you may have noticed that water exits drains swirling in a counter-clockwise pattern. Your knowledge of geography places Sao Paulo in the southern hemisphere. Furthermore, you may have some memory from high school physics class that explains this phenomenon. The earth's rotation and the *law of gravity* do indeed require water to exit drains in Sao Paulo in a direction opposite from what we normally observe. (Okay, that was a little deceptive!)

Two. Again, your strainer is telling you that this statement is ridiculous. If the bite of a cow were deadly, wouldn't you see a little more precaution being used by dairy farmers? Wouldn't you expect to see those who milk or feed cows to be wearing protective gear?

Someone may add a little information to your strainer that may make you question what you know, however. A cow's digestive system is different than ours. Food is partially digested in the first two of the cow's "stomachs," then regurgitated into the mouth to be rechewed. We call this, "chewing the cud." Since a great many bacteria are found in these first two digestive chambers, a cow bite might introduce these bacteria into the body of one bitten.

Finally, though, you may get additional data. Cows have no front upper teeth! To get bitten by a cow one would have to be deeply inside the cows muzzle, and even then, the teeth found there are designed to grind and crush, not to cut. So we can breathe easily. A killer cow rampage is simply not going to happen!

Our amassed knowledge gained from experience, common sense, and education makes up our strainer. We use it to make a judgment about the soundness of a particular idea before accepting it as fact. That which we accept becomes a permanent part of our store of knowledge and is used to strain new data. That's the way the strainer works.

But let's go back to number three. Our knowledge of the biology of reproduction tells us that virginity and pregnancy are mutually exclusive! Sexual experience is required for conception. But information beyond biology is in our strainers as Christians. We accept the fact that God was able to waive that prerequisite in the case of Mary. As Christians, we recognize that while other sources of information contain partial truth, the Bible is fully trustworthy. Therefore, we allow God's Word to be the final judge of truth.

I will expand on a point I made earlier: If our mission is to help children and young people prepare to meet the world, there is no lesson more important than to teach them how to use a strainer. Furthermore, we must help our charges to construct strainers that are reinforced with the strong fiber of Scripture.

Now that you have nodded your endorsement, I need to issue a warning. This is a hard lesson to teach, and it comes with a risk involved. In order to teach our children how to distinguish between good ideas and bad ones, we need to let them meet some bad ideas. That's a scary thought. Wouldn't it just be simpler to protect them from bad ideas—to lock them in the basement and not let them come in contact with any thought that might corrupt them? Regardless of what we might think of the feasibility of that approach, it still intrigues us. For example, I don't want my children to endorse Darwin's concepts of the beginning and development of the universe. I have two options. I could protest to their science teachers at school. I could make a big statement and demand my rights as a taxpayer. Or I could decide that they really need to know what Darwin said. They need to study the concepts, to analyze the points one by one, and to strain them through credibility and Biblical truth. The problem with that second option is that someone will have to teach what the Bereans knew—how to use the Bible as a strainer. That is one huge challenge to both parents and their teachers at church. Wouldn't it just be simpler to protect young people from Darwin's theories and hope that they never have to consider them?

Since we are already on a controversial topic, let's hit another issue. I have raised my children in a good Christian home. I have taught them well. I have been a good model. I have watched them develop their devotional lives. Thus, I know that my children will be free of any sexual thoughts until they are at least 21 years old. I know that about my own children, but I am not so sure about yours. Your children need some deliberate, purposeful instruction about their sexual feelings. Of course, I was teasing about my own children. They need that instruction too. I just don't want to face the responsibility of teaching the lesson. Every day our children are bombarded with thousands of ideas about human sexuality, and most of them are wrong. They get ideas from watching T.V. Even the so-called news programs are filled with graphic sexual talk and instructions. Children get ideas from the books and magazines. Even in our newspapers, much of the material is based on the assumption that the reader has a basic understanding of human sexuality. Our children get ideas from their friends. In a typical week, our children will meet more ideas about sexuality than most of us met during our entire childhood and adolescence. Unfortunately, most of those ideas constitute mental and moral trash.

As I said before, my first impulse is to protect my children from hearing all these ideas. I will just find a place where they will never have to deal with them—will never have to strain out the good from the bad, I know I can't do that, and neither can you. The painful reality is that our children need instruction on sexuality.

But who wants to be the teacher? That's the problem. Their friends? The movies they watch? Their school teachers? Their parents? Their teachers at church? However we answer that question, we know that somehow our children are going to have to learn to use the skill of distinguishing between what the world says about sex and what the Bible says. We just can't ignore the reality that our own children and our students are making serious decisions every day. It is imperative that we help them develop the tool of that particular decision-making process. In other words, they need strainers.

This lesson of learning to strain wouldn't be so difficult if all bad ideas came to us wearing warning labels, "Attention! This is a bad idea. Letting this idea permeate your thoughts and direct your decisions and actions could be dangerous to your spiritual health!" But the bad ideas don't come with labels. Often they come to us as attractive alternatives, appealing and handsome, and they often come to us when we least expect them. Darwin's theory of evolution serves as a good example. When our students are in biology, they are listening for that idea. They have their strainer up and working. If they hear a Darwinian point, they will probably recognize it and will know how to strain it.

But what if they hear a Darwinian idea in a history or psychology class? C. S. Lewis bumped into a dangerous, semi-Darwinian idea in a grammar book, and he was moved to write his classic *The Abolition of Man* as a warning to all of us about how subtly bad ideas can seep into our thoughts and, consequently, the thoughts of a whole society. This activity of straining requires constant vigilance.

Another other problem with bad ideas is that they come from a multitude of seemingly innocent and attractive sources. For years, I have been amused at how much confidence students have in their textbooks—or the "holy" books, as I call them. On occasions, I have had to tell adolescents that their textbook contains an error. That is not a pleasant duty. Oh! The arguments that follow!

In recent weeks, this issue has passed beyond amusing. As I write this, I am teaching in a university in China. The textbook I am using for my class in American studies was written by a Chinese person who never visited America. The book is filled with simply false information and outdated material. The scary part comes from the inferences and implications of the subtle propaganda written by a person with ideologies and a belief system different from mine. How do I teach these sharp, young Chinese minds how to find the truth and strain out both the blatant false information and the subtle lies found on almost every page? What is one teacher's voice against the power of a textbook? Will they strain my ideas as well as those of the textbook?

We also get bad ideas from people. Although it was Paul who was coming to speak, the Bereans still took out their Bibles to strain his sermon. I like that response. I appreciate experts. I really appreciate teachers. I respect their wisdom and knowledge, but I still need to remember that those experts are human, subject to human error. When I hear the expert speak, I need to know enough about the infallible word of God that I can use it to strain out any possible human error. One of the unfortunate frailties of too many of us is that we have too much respect for those people in our lives that we have appointed as our experts.

A few years ago, our family moved into a new community and joined a church. As newcomers and as naturally shy people, we found a corner near the back and worshiped in basic anonymity, speaking to no more than four or five others per week. After about two months, the deacons asked me to be the interim pastor. I moved from the back row to the pulpit, and I immediately became the world's foremost expert on every human matter. "Pastor, how do I get along with my neighbor?" "Pastor, how should I wear my hair?" "Pastor, where can I find a Christian doctor?"

Frankly, I was frightened when I realized how much power experts have in our lives. Oh, how we need to learn to use the Bible as a strainer! I was reminded of a commercial only we old-timers will remember, "Which cigarette do you smoke, Doctor?" We now see the irony in that, and we are amused. But it is not too funny to think of how many young people might have started the habit of smoking on the testimony of an expert.

Now that we come to appreciate the need of a strainer, I probably have the duty of discussing the technique of teaching it. Actually, that discussion is a book in itself, but I will summarize it here in two questions which we should regularly incorporate in our teaching.

1) What new ideas have you met this week?

By asking this question, we teach our students to realize that we are exposed to new ideas all the time, and some come quite subtly. When we watch a violent movie, we are exposed to the filmmaker's view of the worth of human life. When we watch a movie showing an adulterous affair, we get the producer's opinion of marriage vows. We need to recognize that we are being exposed to other people's opinions.

2) What does the Bible say about that idea?

That's what the Bereans taught us to ask.

Chapter 11

Fly Under Their Radar

2 Samuel 12:1-14

123

"Then Nathan said to David, 'You are the man!'"

2 Samuel 12:7

"Adolescents . . . are experts at rationalizing their behavior when they are confronted directly. I suspect we all are."

125

"The Lord sent Nathan to David. When he came to him, he said, 'There were two men in a certain town, one rich and the other poor. The rich man had a very large number of sheep and cattle, but the poor man had nothing except one little ewe lamb he had bought. He raised it, and it grew up with him and his children. It shared his food, drank from his cup and even slept in his arms. It was like a daughter to him.

"'Now a traveler came to the rich man, but the rich man refrained from taking one of his own sheep or cattle to prepare a meal for the traveler who had come to him. Instead, he took the ewe lamb that belonged to the poor man and prepared it for the one who had come to him.'

"David burned with anger against the man and said to Nathan, 'As surely as the Lord lives, the man who did this deserves to die! He must pay for that lamb four times over, because he did such a thing and had no pity.'

"Then Nathan said to David, 'You are the man!'"

2 Samuel 12:1-7

The next time you start thinking your teaching assignment is challenging, try Nathan's on for size. One morning you wake up with the assignment (from God) of showing the king that he is a sinner. This isn't just any king. This is King David: adored, admired, and beloved. King David, the military genius; King David, who led his people in worship; King David, the valiant and brave; King David, with the sensitive heart of a poet; King David, appointed to his leadership position by God himself. And you have to teach him that he is a sinner and will have to suffer the consequences! Another thought to consider is that your student is the one person in the kingdom who can order your head to be separated from your body if he reacts badly to the lesson. How is that for challenging?

There are days when you wonder why you ever decided to teach. There are days when you think about calling in sick and letting the substitute take over. There are days when you think it would be easier just to change churches, or even find another job and move out of town.

For me, there was a day in late November when the students returned from lunch in shock from the news that the President had been killed in Dallas. There was a Sunday I taught an adult class the day after the bright, dynamic class president had been arrested for embezzlement. There was a Sunday I taught the fourth grade class after they had all attended the funeral of a classmate who had been killed by a baseball. Of course, the boy who threw the ball was in class that morning. There was the time I substituted in a junior high boys Sunday school class because their regular teacher had stolen money from his company and fled the city with his secretary.

There are times in our teaching career when conventional human wisdom is not enough, and we wonder how we ever got into such a predicament. During those times, I always turn back to 2 Samuel and read about Nathan. On the day of his special lesson, he had two choices. He could have used the direct approach. "Sit down King David; I have a serious lesson to teach you—specifically for you and nobody else. It's like this. King David you are a sinner, and you are going to pay the price."

Instead, Nathan chose the "stealth bomber" approach. He flew in under King David's radar, positioned himself strategically, and then chose the exact moment to drop a payload of truth. This method is nothing short of inspired genius. In all the books and journal articles I have ever read, I have never encountered a better teaching strategy than this. This is teaching at its finest.

I have often wondered what story-telling techniques Nathan used. I wonder what gestures he used. I wonder about his intonation. I wonder if he acted it out. I wonder if he used flannel graph or maybe even a transparency. The little fable itself seems so innocent—a simple tale of the conflict between the common people and the powerful.

Whatever Nathan did, he undoubtedly did it well because he held his class captive, totally involved. This was more than a lesson of words. This was more than a lesson about character development or plot structures or poetic devices. Student David related. He burned with anger. He lost himself in the story. From the position of his leadership role, he even rendered appropriate judgment.

But David didn't know that he was the lesson, that he was the antagonist in the story and that he was rendering judgment upon himself. He did not know the extent to which he was the active participant in the learning process. For lack of a name in educational jargon, I will call what Nathan did simply "the method of unexplained participation." This method offers a shelf full of possible applications for us.

Let's suppose we have a class full of people who just won't talk. Students seem interested enough. They seem to have read their lessons. They seem to like each other. They just won't speak out to discuss the lesson regardless of how good our questions are. (Incidentally this situation has no age boundary. It can happen with nine year olds and ninety year olds.) The direct approach hasn't worked, so now it's time to take a page out of Nathan's method book. At the beginning, we give the class some little written activity. We ask them to rate or rank solutions to a problem, or we might even ask them to write down their thoughts about topics. By asking them to write, we have encouraged each student to form an opinion, to take a side, to justify a decision.

Now that we have them involved that far, we open up the class for discussion, assured that each student should be able to participate because he or she has already formed an opinion. For example, if our lesson for today is about Jesus the comforter, we could begin by telling the class, "Imagine that you have learned that your friend who lives some distance away from you has just discovered that she has cancer. Let's suppose that you can send her only one Bible verse. What one verse will you send? Write out your answer and explain why you chose that verse."

After the students have responded to your prodding to make a decision, they should be able to share their answers with the class; and presto! You have a discussion under way. They didn't expect to participate quite so openly, but they find themselves more involved then they planned to be.

Let's suppose that we have a student or even a whole class of students who need to have more confidence in themselves. Educational methods books devote whole chapters to the virtues of building students' confidence, and they offer us a variety of techniques to accomplish that goal. We can compliment them, or write warm comments on their papers, or call them by name, or take other opportunities to use words to reinforce their self-confidence. We could try the direct approach. We could reprimand them for their lack of confidence, and assure them that we believe in them. That approach may work, but most likely will not. Maybe it is time for us to try the method of unexplained participation. We build one point of the lesson or maybe the whole lesson around something a student said to us. We take his point as the focus, at least for a few minutes. Nothing reinforces a student's sense of self worth more deeply and more powerfully than to use his idea as a springboard for a class activity.

For years, I have been in the habit of writing a quotation on the board each class period. I call it a habit because that is what it is by now. No big deal. No earthshaking methodological discovery. I just write a quotation on the board; something pertinent to the lesson or something about life, or something that has moved me. I use quotations from classical literature and from everyday life. I don't propose this as a teaching requirement. It is just one of the little things that contribute to the lesson, and I think that if I do enough of the little things, maybe the whole lesson will have merit.

Sometimes I will use something a student said as the quotation for the day. So right beside Ben Franklin and Mark Twain and Dr. Dobson, I quote Michael or Michelle. Without expecting it, they become an integral part of the lesson. Nothing I have ever done has more positive reinforcement value than this simple activity.

This simple technique can be applied in many ways in our lessons. When the students least expect it, we will use their ideas and they will become more of a part of the lesson than they had planned. Not only do they learn, they also gain confidence.

For another application of Nathan's method, let's suppose that we have for some reason inherited the unpleasant task of admonishing a class for some wrong behavior. We could use the direct approach. Come to class, stand behind the desk and deliver a prepared speech about why their behavior was wrong and why they shouldn't do it again. Of course, when we use this approach, we need to realize that we will have to fight against their barriers. As soon as we start our speech, the students will get all their defenses up. Of course, I usually teach adolescents, and they are experts at rationalizing their behavior when they are confronted directly; but I suspect we all are, so the indirect method is appropriate for teachers of all ages.

Knowing that mental barriers will fly up at the first indication that students are being rebuked, we may want to imitate Nathan and take a more indirect approach. Involve the students. Engage their attention in a peripheral point, and choose the right moment to zero in on the errant behavior.

Recently one of my students told me of an incident from her own high school career. Several of her classmates had cheated on an exam. During the exam itself, the young teacher said nothing and the students assumed that they had gotten by with their crime. The next day, the teacher came to class, stood behind the teacher's desk, stared at the group, and said absolutely nothing for ten minutes. Resounding, painful, ear-piercing silence filled the room as students and teacher looked at each other. Finally, she spoke softly. She admonished the culprits and announced their punishment. By now, there were no barriers, no rationalizations, no defenses. The silence had been too loud, and in that silence the students had actually participated in their own rebuke. Quite often a simple observation spoken almost off handedly while the students are involved in another point of the lesson can have more corrective power than a ten-minute lecture when they expect it.

Let's suppose we want to teach a moral point. Again we might want to borrow from Nathan, using not only his method, but even his technique of wrapping the point in a fable.

Several years ago, I saw the movie *To Kill a Mockingbird*. As I watched the movie about a trial of an accused black man in a Southern town, I said to myself, "This is a movie about prejudice—about *their* prejudice." I became rather judgmental about prejudiced people. A side story in the movie is about a man named Boo Radley who lived with a mental disability. For most of the film, we learn about him only through the children's reports, and we assume that he is dangerous, harsh, and cruel. When we finally see him, we discover that Boo Radley is a tender, gentle man, and a protector of the children.

Several days after I had seen the film, I suddenly came face-to-face with an ugly truth that I didn't want to admit; this was not a movie about *their* prejudice, it was a movie about *my* prejudice. When I heard the word "mental," I just assumed that Boo Radley was dangerous, harsh, and cruel. At that point, I realized that I had some prejudices too, and that I must deal with those before I became judgmental of others. That's the way the unexplained participation method works. I learned more from that movie than I intended to learn. While listening to a story that I thought was about someone else, I learned something about myself.

That's what Nathan accomplished with his fable the day he went to teach the king that he was a sinner. As an astute teacher, you are probably about ready to wave a yellow flag at this point. "Wait!" you protest. "This does sound like an excellent way to teach, but it's all based on the student getting the point. What if he misses it entirely?" In that protest lies both the beauty and the danger of the method of unexplained participation. To be successful, the method requires each student to participate. He has to bring his own experience and his own thoughts to the learning process. He has to become mentally and emotionally active. He has to be involved.

The most beautiful moment of teaching is when the student becomes involved. We even have a term for it—the teachable moment. It is that special moment when each student lets down his or her guard and becomes an active, even excited, participant in the learning process. At that moment, such an expression of joy glows in their faces that the whole classroom lights up, and we humbly say, "Thank you, God, for allowing me to be a teacher." And we eagerly begin to prepare for the next class.

But what happens if the students don't get it? That is the risk involved with this method. There is something comfortable about the procedure of telling the class to list the three major points of the text with four sub points each. There is is something comfortable about the procedure of transferring the information from our notebooks to their notebooks. There something comfortable about the procedure of having them recite the books of the Bible in order. Not much risk involved in this! We teachers know specifically what we are trying to accomplish. We can watch the lesson unfold step-by-step. We can measure our progress. This is comfortable teaching and *can be* effective education.

But someday, there will come that special challenge when comfortable teaching won't accomplish the objective. Nathan's lesson that day was too important for him to settle for the comfortable approach. He had to take a risk. He had to try a new approach. Of course, the result was positive. We will never know what would have happened if King David had missed the point. But, fortunately for David' soul and for his kingdom, he got the point. And for us, Nathan's lesson becomes an example of teaching at its best.

Not only do we learn how to use the method from Nathan, but we also should gain the confidence to be prepared to take the risk should the seriousness of the situation ever demand it.

Chapter 12

Questions, Anyone?

Matthew 16:13-16

"Who do people say the Son of Man is?"

Matthew 16:13

"We will never know for sure that our students have processed our lessons until we hear the words come out of their mouths."

139

 *"When Jesus came to the region of Caesarea Philippi, he asked his disciples, 'Who do people say the Son of Man is?' "They replied, 'Some say John the Baptist; others say Elijah; and still others, Jeremiah or one of the prophets.' "'But what about you?' he asked. 'Who do you say I am?' "Simon Peter answered, 'You are the Christ, the Son of the living God.'"*

Matthew 16:13-16

"How do I learn how to ask good questions?" the prospective teacher asked.

"One way I could really improve my teaching is to develop my skill in asking questions," the veteran teacher reported.

To both I give the same advice: study the four Gospels. When we discuss Jesus as the Master Teacher, we almost always focus on his ability to relate to his students and his development of lessons through parables. While we can learn a great deal from the Master in both of these areas, studying the parables also allows us to see how and why to ask questions.

Jesus used questions for a whole variety of reasons:

• to discover what the disciples knew
• to test the disciples' faith

- to check the honesty of his students
- to reason with opponents in debates
- to silence his accusers.

As teachers, we know the value of asking questions as a part of our instruction, but we also know that the art of asking good questions is one of the most difficult techniques to develop. When the questioning technique works, the lesson is good; but when the questioning technique fails, the echo of the plunge into failure is so loud that it could drown out our enthusiasm to ever teach again.

Recognizing the difficulty of mastering the art of teaching through questions and then recognizing the peril of not doing it well, the educational experts have worked long and hard at providing us with types of questions, devoting whole books to the topic. There are videos showing a questioning lesson in session. Theories and strategies and instructions are presented and debated in educational literature. But in all this literature, I find the same insights that we learn from Jesus, so when studying the field of questioning, I prefer to go directly to the primary source—to the Gospel account of the Master at work.

The experts tell us that there are different kinds of questions, and questions can be labeled according to the mental activity required to answer them. Some experts argue that there are seven different kinds of mental activity or seven levels of thinking. Others say there are six skills. Still others have reduced the number to four.

Regardless of how many levels of mental activities we may think there are, Jesus included them all in these two questions: "Who do people say the Son of Man is?" "Who do you say I am?" Within these questions is a whole package of tips on the art of using questions in our own classroom.

The Reporting Question

Jesus started this particular class with a rather simple type of question that required the students to assemble some information in their minds and report it. "Who do people say the Son of Man is?" That's easy enough; straightforward and to the point. The students understand what they have been asked to do: remember what they have heard and give it to the teacher either word-for-word or putting the answer in their own language. They don't have to make anything up. They don't have to create or analyze. They just report, knowing that there is definite, correct answer to the question.

In this instance, Jesus' students probably picked up the correct answer through personal, informal research—hanging around on street corners listening to the rumors. Our students may get the correct answers to reporting questions from a variety of sources. They read a book which had been assigned to them. They may have learned the facts in an earlier class. We might have told them the information ourselves. However they gained the knowledge, we think that it is important for them to have it. We ask the questions to see if they have retained the knowledge. But asking reporting questions fills more purposes than that.

• **Process the information**

Reporting questions let us know whether or not students have processed the information for themselves. We can study their eyes looking for the glint of cognition. We can study their body language looking for the calm and ease that says, "I understand," but we will never know for sure that our students have processed our lessons until we hear the words come out of their mouths. When we realize our purpose in asking reporting questions, these questions are not hard to phrase or to administer. We simply ask the students to put into words what we want them to know. "Name the twelve disciples." "In what book do we find the Sermon on the Mount?" "Who was Jacob's brother?" "How was David related to his enemy Absalom?"

After we have asked the question, we pick out a student to answer. We could choose the one with his hand up yelling, "Me, me!" We could choose the quiet one in the corner. We could go up and down the row. Regardless of how we do it, it is probably more effective to choose a specific student rather than throw questions out to let the class scramble for an answer. That's the technique. Just that simple, but it is so valuable in our teaching because we need to know if our students can verbalize the information.

• Check the attention level

Reporting questions help us know if the students are listening. If we are giving a lecture, we never know for sure who is listening and who is comprehending, so we need to pause at least once every five minutes to ask one of the reporting questions of some specific student. Again, this is the only way we know for sure if the class is tuned in or whether we have explained it clearly. Asking the direct questions to specific students is far more effective than some alternatives, such as constantly asking, "OK? OK? or "Do you see that?" or even the infamous, "Are there any questions?" Not too long ago I caught myself asking this question to a classroom of sober faces, and I was reminded again of what a worthless utterance it is. Of course they had questions, but they didn't understand the principle well enough to put their questions into words. They were waiting for me to form questions for them to answer to show me how close they were to comprehending. That's the way we check to see whether or not we presented the information clearly and they have understood what we said.

Recently I visited an eighth-grade class to watch a young teacher cover the topic of family structure. For ten minutes he presented an excellent explanation of monogamy— not only describing it thoroughly and giving appropriate examples, but also endorsing the positive merits of such an arrangement. He was good—enthusiastic, animated, and in tune with those eighth graders. Being a knowledgeable teacher, he paused at the proper moment and checked for comprehension. He asked with an encouraging tone, "What do you call it when one woman and one man are married to each other all their lives?"

"That's called monotony," Sarah answered confidently.

• Activate the minds

We ask reporting questions to stimulate the thinking processes of our students. Jesus could have started his class with a short lecture. "The people are rather confused about who I am. They have the idea that I an someone special, but they don't know where I fit in the scene of their history and theology. Some think that I am John the

Baptist returned to life after being beheaded. Others think that I might be Elijah. Some have guessed Jeremiah. Some people think that I am one of the prophets, although they aren't sure which one." From what we know about Jesus, we can assume that he knew what people were saying, but he wanted to hear it from his students. Asking them achieved two goals: he learned what they knew, and he got them involved in the process. They weren't sitting passively. Their minds were working. They were involved in the lesson and were prepared for the next step.

We can learn a great deal from Jesus here. A good question at the beginning of the class gets the students' minds working, and could make a great contribution to how much they learn that day.

• Build their confidence

We asked reporting questions to build the confidence of our students. I imagine that the disciples were rather pleased with themselves after they had answered Jesus' question. "Great!" they may have thought, " I just answered the Master's question; I'm a part of what's going on."

We sometimes tell ourselves that *our* students don't like questions. We see other teachers successfully using questions in their teaching, but we don't use questions because our students don't enjoy them. That isn't true. What students dislike are questions they can't answer, but they enjoy questions they can answer. This observation applies not just to those who teach children and adolescents. I often visit adults classes where distinguished people raise their hands, and, in effect, shout "Me! Me!"

Most students do enjoy answering questions when they know the answer, and having them tell us what they know is a good way to convince them they can learn the lesson.

• Open students' minds

We ask reporting questions at the beginning to get out the tools our students will need for the rest of the lesson. From this text, we gather that Jesus' main purpose was not to find out what people thought of him, but to move his class to the real lesson—a statement of their personal faith. Timing is imperative. We don't walk into class right at the bell and ask, "What is the nature of God?" or "What is the meaning of the universe?" To open the doors to the inner depths of our students' minds, we have to use some preliminary tools. I know this sounds a bit exaggerated, but we make this mistake more often than we may think we do. We read a story together and then ask, "Did you like the story?" That should be the last question of the day. Our students aren't prepared to analyze their feelings about the story, or their relationship to the story, until we have asked some preliminary questions. To get our students to think deeply about an issue or to analyze a situation or to make an intelligent judgment, we first must prime their mental operations with a question that they can answer successfully. *Help them* analyze their thoughts and feelings. *Help them* form a clear and supportable opinion.

With his first question, Jesus found out what the disciples knew, he got them involved in the process, he built up their confidence, and he engaged their minds for the rest of the lesson. What great results from one little question!

The Penetrating Question:

Now, Jesus was ready to ask the second question, to move to the next level of the lesson, to take his class into a new dimension of their spiritual development. "But what about you? Who do you say I am?" This question required the class to remember the information they had learned, to organize it, analyze it, check its validity against their own knowledge, and then to dig into themselves to discover their own personal perspective and their own commitment. To answer Jesus' second question they had to use all their levels of thinking and all types of mental activity. The genius of Jesus' lesson plan was that his students were now ready for this step. They could answer this question!

And what a beautiful answer it was—succinct and thorough. How I pray that each of my students might answer that question with the same straightforward confidence Peter showed when he said, "You are the Christ, the Son of the living God."

How pleased Jesus must have been when he heard those words and could pronounce his endorsement of Peter's answer! How pleased Jesus must be when any one of us comes to the point in our understanding where we can make our personal leap to faith!

This one example of Jesus' teaching gives us both great instruction on how to use reporting questions, and the joy of the doxology when students successfully answer questions that require them to analyze, create, evaluate, and believe. And therein lies the difference between good teaching and great teaching; good teaching incorporates the first type of question and great teaching dares to include both.

"I want to teach my students *how* to think and not just *what* to think," we have all said at one time in our teaching careers; and we are concerned about whether we are helping our students develop critical thinking skills and problem-solving techniques. We know that we need to move beyond the process of storing information in student brains and occasionally asking them to relay it back, but venturing into

149

the second type of question is not only difficult, it is also daring.

For one thing, asking students to create their own answer strips them of their security. As we said earlier, almost all students enjoy answering questions when they know the answers. This is safe and even rewarding. Now we dare to ask them a question for which there is no specific answer. At this point, they look at us as if to say, "Please tell me what you want me to say. I don't know what I think until you tell me what to think."

I often wake up in the middle of the night with visions of twenty-five pairs of eyes staring at me, clearly communicating the pain and fear of not knowing how to answer my question. That's what I call a nightmare. I do sometimes think that it would be easier to drop that whole enterprise and just ask the type of questions that produce security and smiles and waving hands.

Analytical questions are also hard to form. Maybe that is why we don't use them as often as we should. It is easy to ask our students to tell us what they know. It is much more difficult to phrase a question or an activity that asks them what they think or even what they believe. It is easy to ask students where to find the Beatitudes. It is difficult to formulate a question that causes them to think about how the Beatitudes affect their daily decisions and actions. It is easy to ask students to list the kings of Israel. It is difficult to build a question that asks them what we learn from these kings to make us more responsible citizens. It is easy to ask them to list the reasons why the children of Israel complained so much in the wilderness. It is difficult to formulate a question that asks them whether Moses was a good leader in the way he handled the complaining horde.

We develop the art of asking the deeper, soul-searching questions through trial and error. There are no magic tips from a textbook guaranteeing success or your money cheerfully refunded. To move our class to this next level of learning, we must take a risk, step into the unknown. Sometimes the questions work, and our efforts are reinforced by the joy of victory. Sometimes the questions flop, and we learn from the agony of defeat. Through years of trial and error, I have learned a great deal about the process of constructing those questions. While I *don't* enjoy success with greater regularity, I *have* developed the skill of dealing with the failure!

A fine example of the question that makes us think is the W.W.J.D material presently sweeping the world. I first found that question, "What would Jesus do?" in one of the most powerful books I have ever read, *In His Steps,* by Charles M. Sheldon. In his book, the question changed the attitude and life of an entire community. Every time I see someone wearing a W.W.J.D. bracelet, I wonder if that person has been moved to think deeply about the question, and how he or she has responded to it. The power of such an introspective question is that it can move your class to a new dimension of personal commitment—just as Jesus' questions moved his class to a commitment that changed the world.

Chapter 13

The Might
of the Metaphor

Psalm 23

"The Lord is my shepherd."

Psalm 23:1

"The concept takes shape and is permanently etched into our minds, providing us with a clear image of our eternal Father."

155

Have you ever wondered why so many people know the twenty-third Psalm? When someone begins to recite this passage, even people who have very little knowledge of God's Word begin moving their lips, forming the words. Have you ever noticed how a sense of awe and peace falls over the group at this point?

In 1991, Mary and I taught in a university in Kiev, Ukraine, just as that nation was emerging from the Soviet Union and developing its own independence. On Thanksgiving Day, I was scheduled to teach a lecture class of approximately two hundred students and professors. I wasn't too excited about the opportunity. After all, it was Thanksgiving. I should be home giving thanks, feasting, and watching T.V. I had never taught on Thanksgiving Day before. Of course, the Ukrainians didn't know anything about Thanksgiving. To them it was just another day. I decided that for my mental health, I would start the class with a Bible reading. That's one privilege of being a teacher; once in a while, we can use class time to do something just for ourselves. I chose Psalm 23. With an auditorium full of people just coming out of seventy years of communism and atheism and all the required propaganda, I wasn't too sure how to approach the subject. Rather timidly, I told them that I would read an ancient Hebrew poem. As I started "The Lord is my shepherd," I saw their lips begin to move, forming the words. All over the auditorium, they joined in—some in English, some in Russian. That Thanksgiving Day I stood at the front of the auditorium and heard a stereophonic recitation of Psalm 23—in two languages. I have no idea how, where, or why those people learned it, but they knew it, and their recitation turned that day into an unforgettable Thanksgiving.

How do you account for the power and the popularity of this one poem located in the midst of 149 other poems much like it? Of course, it is beautiful poetry—well-written and pleasant to the ear, but I believe there is another dimension at work here. This metaphoric poem is an extremely effective way to teach the beauty and majesty of God's loving care for each individual.

We could use many words to describe God: majestic, supreme, sovereign, omniscient, loving—those are good words valuable to our understanding. But when we hear the metaphor, "The Lord is my shepherd," something else happens to us. We form in our minds the picture—distinct and unforgettable—of the Lord Jesus carrying a helpless lamb. The image is so clear that it has become a favorite subject for painters. In fact as I traveled across Ukraine after that memorable Thanksgiving Day, I saw many paintings of God the Shepherd. Through those simple words, the concept takes shape and is permanently etched into our minds, providing us a clear image of our eternal Father. Not only does the metaphor teach us right now, but it continues to teach day in and day out throughout our lives. We will never forget the picture. There is yet another dimension to the lesson. Not only do we get a description of God, but from that image we learn how we should respond to such a being. I once heard of a little girl who recited her memory verse, "The Lord is my shepherd. That is all I want." She may have been a bit confused about the words, but it seems to me that she had good insight into the theology.

As sheep in God's pasture, we can romp and gambol and nibble knowing full well that we are never beyond his care and protection. If we should get out of his line of sight, he will come looking for us. We will lie down in a safe haven when we are tired; and when it comes time for us to move through the valley, we can go with the confidence that the Shepherd is with us all the way. That's what it means to be a sheep in God's pasture. Have you ever thought of how many people throughout history have learned the lesson of who God is through the power of this poetic metaphor?

The implication to those of us who teach is obvious; we need to use metaphors to make our concepts clear and lasting. Years before most of you were born, my excellent high school English teacher, Mrs. Simmons, taught me about prepositions by using the metaphor of a cat and a box. She held a box in one hand and a stuffed cat in the other. Then she demonstrated all the relationships of prepositions—over, under, beside, in, out, near. Through the years, as I taught hundreds of students about prepositions by using a cat and a box, I did wonder how Mrs. Simmons came up with such a brilliant lesson, but I was sure that she and I were the only teachers who knew about it. Then I visited schools in Ukraine and discovered that English teachers there teach prepositions by using the cat and the box. Then I visited schools in China, and I saw the same lesson. That metaphor is used worldwide, just as effectively as it was years ago in a rural school in western Oklahoma. At this point, you are probably saying, "This all sounds wonderful. I see the value of metaphorical teaching, but I don't know how to write a metaphor appropriate for every lesson. King David wrote Psalm 23, but he was a poet with a poet's ability to express himself in pictures. What do I do?"

The good news is that we don't have to write all the metaphors. We have help. The Bible is filled with them—wonderful, well-written descriptions of ideas almost too profound for words. For example, in the Gospel of John, we find a metaphor for Jesus in almost every chapter: Jesus is the Word, the Lamb of God, the Water of Life, the Bread of Life, the Way, the Good Shepherd, the Vine, the Truth, and the Resurrection. We could build almost a year of lessons on those alone.

Recently I attended an educational conference where noted scholars presented their research findings on effective teaching methods. One scholar spoke of metaphorical teaching. Using scientific terms and charts and graphics he showed how our minds process information into pictures efficiently at those times when we need to remember. It was a good presentation—analytical, persuasive, and well-documented. This noted scholar verified what I had already suspected because I have seen the teaching power of Psalm 23. About the only problem with the presentation was that the scholar needed a solid example of metaphorical teaching as a summary point. I could have given him a suggestion. Turning once more in that great methods book, we find that Paul wanted to teach the Ephesians the lesson of the depth and breadth and intensity of Jesus' love for us. This is a tough concept—one that almost goes beyond language and even pushes the limits of our human minds to comprehend. For a lesson this important, this powerful, and this deep, Paul found an appropriate metaphor: husbands and wives. Every time I read Ephesians 5:22-33, I get a very clear picture.

"I love you," I tell Mary.

"How much?" she wants to know.

Now what do I do? Stand there with my hands outstretched as if I am measuring a fish I just caught? How much do I love my bride? How do I describe it in words? How much I love Mary is just the beginning of how much my heavenly Bridegroom loves me. The picture is clear. The lesson is effective. What a great way to teach!

But Paul wasn't finished with just one lesson from the metaphor. He then turned it around and taught two lessons with the same image. In teaching me how much Jesus loves me, he teaches me how much I am to love Mary and how I am to show that love every moment of every day just as Jesus shows his love for me every moment of every day. The lesson is clear and convincing.

This passage is so effective in creating the instructional picture in my mind that I almost overlook the brilliance of the teaching strategy. In a few short sentences, Paul, by using a two-sided metaphor, teaches one of the most effective lessons I have ever learned—a lesson that brings me joy every minute of every day. I wonder if Paul could recite Psalm 23.

Chapter 14

First, a
History Lesson

Acts 7

"Was there ever a prophet your fathers did not persecute?"

Acts 7:52

"One of the haunting problems of teaching in a church setting is the wide range of knowledge and experience among the learners."

 If you ever get the urge to complain that you have a tough class, try slipping into Stephen's sandals—that should give you a new perspective! His "students" weren't merely disinterested. They weren't just pestering their neighbors or whispering. They weren't simply shaking their heads and piercing him with stares that defy authority. No, this crowd was bloodthirsty.

Stephen had to know that he was on trial for his life. He had to know that this just might be his final hour. What inspires me is that, in the face of all this danger, he still seized the opportunity to teach a lesson. That's what teachers do. They teach every chance they get. They turn even a trial for their lives into a classroom for one final lesson.

"To this [Stephen] replied: 'Brothers and fathers, listen to me! The God of glory appeared to our father Abraham while he was still in Mesopotamia, before he lived in Haran. "Leave your country and your people," God said, "and go to the land I will show you." . . .

"'And Abraham became the father of Isaac and circumcised him eight days after his birth. Later Isaac became the father of Jacob, and Jacob became the father ot the twelve patriarchs. . . .

"'As the time drew near for God to fulfill his promise to Abraham, the number of our people in Egypt greatly increased. Then another king, who knew nothing about Joseph, became ruler of Egypt. . . .

"'At that time Moses was born, and he was no ordinary child. . . .

"'Then the Lord said to him, . . . "I have indeed seen the oppression of my people in Egypt. I have heard their groaning and have come down to set them free." . . .

"'But our fathers refused to obey [Moses]. Instead, they rejected him and in their hearts turned back to Egypt. They told Aaron, "Make us gods who will go before us." . . .

"'Our forefathers had the tabernacle of the Testimony with them in the desert.' . . .

"'However, the Most High does not live in houses made by men.' . . .

"'You stiff-necked people, with uncircumcised hearts and ears! You are just like your fathers: You always resist the Holy Spirit!'"

Acts 7:2, 3, 8, 17, 18, 20, 33, 34, 39, 40, 44, 48, 51

Stephen's lesson itself was straightforward and succinct. "You stiff-necked people with uncircumcised hearts and ears. You are just like your fathers." In other words, "You have not learned one thing from history." There is an adage that says that a person who doesn't know his history is doomed to repeat it. Because so many have quoted this, I really don't know to whom to attribute it, but maybe we can trace it all the way back to Stephen because this was the major point of his lesson. The warning had to be delivered, and Stephen was determined to use his last breath to deliver it.

Before Stephen got to the heart of his lesson, he took a step that is the mark of good teaching but a step often overlooked by many of us. He set the lesson up. He introduced his main point with an historical overview. In one speech, Stephen fulfilled two objectives: He presented the background and provided an overview of the lesson for the day. Both of these objectives merit some commentary.

Background:

In this situation, Stephen decided it would be productive to give his class the historical background of the problem—and what a background it was! In what surely took less then five minutes, he covered a few thousand years of Jewish history incorporating the names of the heroes, the major events, and the failures. If someday you need a quick refresher on Old Testament history, just read Stephen's introduction; you'll get the main ideas.

What an effective use of five minutes! But I find it interesting that Stephen saw the need to give this historical background. His class consisted of members of the Sanhedrin. Wouldn't he assume that those guys knew that history already? If I had been the teacher, I would have assumed that, but within that assumption lies a key to ineffective teaching. Too often, we teachers assume that our students know the Bible. We assume that they have heard the stories. We assume that they have read the commentaries. We assume that they understand the terms, and can identify the people. Some of our students probably do have that information, but some don't. We must face every class with the assumption that some of our students don't have the background on which to hang today's lesson, and without that reference point, they are going to have a hard time nailing down the lesson permanently in their minds and lives.

Let's take this present discussion as an example. I have just assumed that all my readers know what the Sanhedrin was, who was in it, and what they did. If you don't have that background, you aren't learning as much from this as you would learn if you had a reference point. You may be feeling a bit incomplete about now. You may even be a bit frustrated. You may feel guilty because I have inferred that you should know something that you don't know. You may have lost some confidence. You may be upset with me and about ready to put the book down.

Welcome to my class! I am sure that I have students who experience all those feelings frequently when I go bursting straight into the material of the class because I have assumed that they have the background.

One of the haunting problems of teaching in a church setting is the wide range of knowledge and experience among the learners found in any one group. We can see this right away with children. We can assume that if our fourth graders have all been in the same school system, they have had about the same amount of experience in math. Some have held onto more math knowledge than others, but they've had about the same exposure. This isn't the case with religious education. Some of those fourth graders have been climbing on Mom's knee for a daily dose of Bible stories for almost ten years. Some have never heard the stories. They want to learn. They want to remember. They want to apply. But they need the background first.

This discovery is obvious in the children's classes, but it is brutal in the adult classes. Statistics tell us how hard it is to win an adult to the kingdom. Most of the people who come to a belief in Christ make that initial decision early in their lives. I don't know all the causes for the alarming statistics, but I do worry about how uncomfortable some adults might be in our classes.

Let's suppose that a forty-year-old couple decides that their whole family needs some experience with this "religion thing." They know they need the moral training, and they suspect that there is something deeper involved. They get up earlier than usual for a Sunday morning, dress the children in their finest, and come to our church. After a frantic search around the building to find an appropriate niche for everyone, Mom and Dad come to our class to settle in for some Bible instruction. Today's lesson is about God's choosing Saul as the first king of Israel. Now put yourself in that new couple's position. Who is Samuel? Who are the Israelites? How does all this apply to modern American morality?

Be honest. If you were in their place would you come back? Now be honest again; if you were in their place, how much better would you have felt about the whole enterprise if I had spent five minutes providing a short background. This illustration is actually current with me. Recently I taught what I thought was a well-planned lesson about Saul's appointment as king. Rather pleased with myself for being such an informed teacher, I was hanging around the room as the people left hoping to pick up a bit if their approval as well. One woman came up and said, "May I ask a question?"

"Well, yes of course," I assured her with my tone that said I had a grasp on wisdom.

"Why is there an old Bible and a new Bible?" she asked. Whoops! I assumed too much. Although I was confident that I had explained the story of the appointment of Israel's first king, I had been totally unsuccessful as far as this woman had been concerned. Though seasoned believers understand the distinction between Old Testament and New Testament history (the "old Bible and a new Bible"), this woman did not. I needed to take a few moments to set the stage. I needed to place the story in the context of history. I needed to review events that had gone before this story and preview those that would follow. This dear woman was confused because I had purposely chosen to skip this background step that day.

But what about the people who do have the Bible background? Won't they be bored? Not if the material is presented well. A concise review of pertinent facts serves as a reminder, and says to them, "Dig out some of that data you have stored in the deep recesses of your mind. We are going to hang today's lesson on it." Both the informed and uninformed alike should find a background report valuable to setting a stage for effective learning.

Overview:

Stephen didn't just present a sound byte of background. In those five minutes, he gave the big picture—the whole thing—the complete story. In other words, he gave an overview. I am a big fan of an overview introduction to lessons. Most of the time my lessons deals with a specific point, a specific date, a specific person, which leads to a specific concept. I can teach that concept with all my energy and with all my creative talents, but if my students don't know how that concept relates to the concepts around it and to the big picture, they will have only a little island of information with absolutely no idea what to do with it.

We can illustrate this point with many examples. We teach students that Washington, D.C. sits between Virginia and Maryland, but they have never seen a map of the United States. We teach students about the Civil War, but they have never seen a timeline of American history. We teach students about degrees of comparison of adjectives, but they can't name the eight parts of speech. In the same way, we teach students about Paul's first missionary journey, but they don't know whether it is found in the Old or New Testament.

This is one of the big red flags of church educational programs. We teach the Bible in bits and pieces, and we expect the students to plug all that data into an appropriate spot in the history of the Christian church. But where do they get the cognitive timeline we assume they have? When do we teach the overview? When do we teach it to children growing up in the church? When do we teach it to adults coming into the church later in life?

If you would like to check me out on this point, save five minutes at the end of the next class and give your students a small test. You can write twenty of these questions in a few minutes: Who came first? Moses or Noah? Saul or Solomon? Moses or Abraham? Elijah or Jeremiah? Barnabas or John the Baptist? Stephen or King David? The answers you get should provide you valuable data about what kind of grasp of the big picture your students have.

Stephen used his last bit of human energy to give his class a historical overview before he got to the main point of the lesson. His efforts were not in vain. At the very least, I am a better teacher because of the method I learned from him.

Chapter 15

Use Their Coin

Matthew 22:15-22

"Show me the coin used for paying the tax."

Matthew 22:19

"Tactile learners use their hands to feed their minds. They have to touch it and hold it and tear it apart."

177

"Then the Pharisees went out and laid plans to trap him in his words. They sent their disciples to him along with the Herodians. 'Teacher,' they said, 'we know you are a man of integrity and that you teach the way of God in accordance with the truth. You aren't swayed by men, because you pay no attention to who they are. Tell us then, what is your opinion? Is it right to pay taxes to Caesar or not?'

"But Jesus, knowing their evil intent, said, 'You hypocrites, why are you trying to trap me? Show me the coin used for paying the tax.' They brought him a denarius, and he asked them, 'Whose portrait is this? And whose inscription?'

"'Caesar's,' they replied.

"Then he said to them, 'Give to Caesar what is Caesar's, and to God what is God's.'"

Matthew 22:15-22

Jesus used their coin. What a brilliant teaching strategy! The Parisees had not come to learn a lesson on taxation, or civic duty, or moral responsibility, or the role of authority in their lives. They had come to accuse, to corner, and to trap. Jesus had to find some way to turn that evil intent into an attitude with enough vulnerability to allow them to learn something. He accomplished his purpose by using their coin!

The first thing Jesus accomplished by using that coin was to accommodate all the different learning styles present in his class, because everyone can learn from an object lesson.

The educational experts tell us that people learn differently. Auditory learners gain most of what they know through the sense of hearing. Visual learners gain most of what they know through the sense of sight. Tactile learners use their hands to feed their minds. They have to touch it and hold it and tear it apart.

Being an educational expert himself, Jesus obviously understood different learning styles because he used different teaching styles to reach every student that day. The auditory learners heard him say, "Give to Caesar what is Caesar's and to God what is God's." The visual learners saw the coin and could see the image of Caesar. The tactile guys held the coin in their hands as they passed it through the crowd up to the teacher.

Allow the coins in your pocket or purse to remind you of this rather disturbing point every time you step into a classroom: students don't learn in the same way. Although their differences are probably too widespread and too complex to fit neatly into three small packages, the three categories of auditory, visual, and tactile learners offer us a place to start. Your students are all sitting there—with all

179

three kinds learning styles, with special joys, and special needs, and they are all precious souls thirsty for the knowledge of God.

There are times when I get the idea that we think all Christians are auditory learners. I've noticed that much of our teaching in church situations employs our mouths and ears. "Sit down, be quiet, and listen to me" is too often the program for the day. I know that I am often guilty.

I call the fact that there are different learning styles disturbing because whenever I pause to analyze what went on in my class, I always feel a twinge of guilt when I ask myself, "What did the tactile learners get from today's lesson?" Sometimes I am rather confident in my ability to teach auditory learners. Sometimes I am even pleased with what I do for the visual learners. It is those tactile learners that I most often leave out.

It does appear that churches are becoming more conscious of the different learning styles among the congregation. Some ministers are now providing visual learners with copies of the outline. Some are using dramatic presentations as a part of the worship service. Have you ever noticed those adults who sit on their edge during a children's sermon with a good object lesson? That in itself should tell us something about the way we learn.

The good news is that once we become aware of the different styles of learning, we can develop tools to help people use their own personal style to maximize their learning ability.

Teenagers frequently tell me that they don't enjoy church. "Why?" I want to know.

"The sermon is boring," they all give the same answer. Yet, I see adults in the same congregation hanging on every word and begging for more when the time is up. The reason for the contradiction is obvious. Those teenagers have not developed the skills to listen to a sermon and learn from it. One of the answers to this problem is to provide teenagers with the necessary tools to outline the sermon. This activity will involve the hands and the eyes as well as the ears. They won't be bored, and they will learn more.

Jesus didn't merely give a lecture on the history of taxation, Roman occupation, and civil duty to stimulate his students' hearing. He used a real coin, and the coin was one he got from his students!

This may seem like a trivial maneuver, but sometimes a small gesture can have a big impact. I once went to hear a well-known, popular preacher. In the middle of his sermon, to clarify a point, he read Philippians 4:4-7 from his *King James Version* pulpit Bible. He then paused and said, "I like the language better in the *New International Version*. Who has an NIV®?" Someone seated in the middle of a crowd of a thousand waved an NIV®. The preacher then left the pulpit, walked off the stage, traveled down the aisle, took the Bible, opened it to the right page, and stood there in the middle of the crowd reading the Scripture. I suspect he had the words memorized and could have recited them flawlessly from his position safely behind his podium. But he didn't do that. He went out into the crowd, and used a Bible from one of us. An insignificant gesture? That was fourteen years ago, and I vividly recall every detail. Do you think the person who handed him the Bible remembers the Scripture he read that day?

Jesus and all the people gathered around him knew whose picture was on their Roman coin, but rather than just talk about it, he asked someone to pull out a coin and hand it to him.

Several years ago, a woman presenting an anti-smoking campaign came to our high school. She had an interesting plastic dummy that smoked a cigarette while its lungs filled up with ugly black tar. It was a vivid, sobering picture with a strong visual lesson. To make the point even stronger, the speaker asked for a cigarette from one of our students. A jovial senior who was not afraid to admit that he carried cigarettes gave her one of his. Right on cue, the dummy smoked the cigarette while his lungs filled up with ugly black tar. The student who had provided the cigarette marched to the front of the room and threw his remaining cigarettes into the wastebasket. His fellow students applauded.

I have no idea whether or not that student kept his resolve to give up smoking, but at least he threw away one package of cigarettes. Would he have done that much if the speaker had used her own cigarette? I don't know, but using a cigarette out of a student's package boosted the learner participation and increased the impact of her point. It did something else as well; by asking for a cigarette from the audience, everyone knew that she was using a typical cigarette, not one created with extra tar for special effect. Magicians often use objects from the audience for this very reason. If using an object from the audience creates extra impact for them, why not for teachers?

Jesus used their coin. Just a single little teaching strategy, but the impact was that the students all walked out of class that day remembering what they had learned.

Chapter 16

Start With the Headlines

Acts 17:16-34

"Men of Athens! I see that in every way you are very religious."

Acts 17:22

"Paul reversed the procedure. He started with TIME magazine and built to the Bible text."

"While Paul was waiting for [Silas and Timothy to join him] in Athens, he was greatly distressed to see that the city was full of idols. So he reasoned in the synagogue with the Jews and the God-fearing Greeks, as well as in the marketplace day by day with those who happened to be there. . . .

"Paul then stood up in the meeting of the Areopagus and said: 'Men of Athens! I see that in every way you are very religious. For as I walked around and looked carefully at your objects of worship, I even found an altar with this inscription: TO AN UNKNOWN GOD. Now what you worship as something unknown I am going to proclaim to you.'"

Acts 17:16, 17, 22, 23

I really enjoy watching a good lesson unfold. It's like listening to an orchestra when all instruments are harmonizing to create a unified melody. Paul's lesson to the Epicurean and Stoic philosophers gathered in Athens is a good example of a lesson as a beautifully composed symphony. All the notes worked together as he took his class through each measure and each movement to one magnificent, rousing finale.

In simple language, we could say that the lesson had an introduction, a body, and a conclusion. That observation in itself is instructive. All good lessons have a definite introduction, body, and conclusion. We may coin different labels and tell ourselves that we have come up with something new in lesson planning order. Currently, the in-the-know educators talk of the anticipatory set, the input step, and closure; but what they are really telling us is that good lessons have an introduction, body, and conclusion. This little insight itself helps us when we plan. If we think in these terms of organization, we know what our task is when we start to plan. One of the greatest time-savers in lesson preparation is to know where we are going before we start. Not only does it save us time, but it also helps create a lesson that unfolds with a sense of harmony and rhythm.

Paul's powerful lesson was presented under some rather tough parameters. He used the simple organizational structure of an introduction, body, and conclusion, but the beauty of his presentation was in how he used each step to communicate with his specific audience.

His introduction is art at its best. I call this the starter. Obviously, every lesson has to start somewhere, but too often, we don't give enough attention to this point in our teaching. The most precious five minutes of any class are the two and a half minutes at the start and the two and a half minutes at the conclusion. Planning the right approach and using those five minutes appropriately is the key to moving our lesson to a whole new level.

Paul had some options for his starter. He could have introduced himself and explained why he was this far from home. He could have read a Bible text. He could have developed the history of the Jewish nation. He could have told those philosophers that Christ died for them. Instead, Paul chose to start with a current events topic. He took a scene familiar to all his students—an idea that would have already been on their minds—a topic from their news.

The older methods books call this the application, and most recommend that we build up to it. In other words, we start with the Bible text and end with *TIME* magazine. In most situations, this is the logical sequence. But for this lesson and for this particular class, Paul revised the procedure. He started with *TIME* magazine and built to the Bible text. When we look at the results, we see the wisdom of his approach. These philosophers came to class with their defenses up. "What does this man have to teach us? We are Athenians. We are enlightened academicians. This man is a foreigner. He can't possibly have anything relevant to say to us. He doesn't know anything about our life here in the great city. He proposes to teach us something about religion. Ha! Look at those statues out there. We know about religion. We have a god for everything. I am sure that regardless of his beliefs, this foreigner doesn't have nearly as many gods as we do. And he is going to teach us about religion?"

Although we may not want to face the fact, we probably have learners in our class with about the same kind of attitude. I call them the "I dare you" crowd. "Here I am at church. I know I should be here. My mother taught me that much. But I'm not really all that interested. I have a real job in a real life. I have real problems in a real world. That Bible you read from was written a long time ago. It's all about holy people—different from me. I dare you. Just once say something about the real world in which I live."

As I prepare my lessons and as I stand in front of my class, I need a constant reminder that the "I dare you" people are sitting there. Some of them come every week, and there may be several of them. Somehow I have to find a way to say to them during that first two and a half minutes, "Yes, you are interested in this lesson. You may not think you are, but you are. This lesson has far more to do with your real world than you could ever imagine."

That's exactly what Paul accomplished with his starter taken from the current events of the day. Look at how artfully he gained their attention: "You are religious. I can see that. Your city has conveyed that to me clearly. I just want to fill you in on the God you already know about—the one you already have an altar to. Let me tell you how I found your Unknown God."

I believe he won their attention and gained the right to teach them, which are two important steps in the teaching process. Sometimes we teachers have to earn our right to teach, particularly with some in the "I dare you" crowd.

Take a moment to look at this part of his address: "God did this so that men would seek him and perhaps reach out for him and find him, though he is not far from each one of us. 'For in him we live and move and have our being.' As some of your own poets have said, 'We are his offspring'" (Acts 17:27, 28).

In a masterful, yet understated way, Paul displayed his intellectual credentials. Very subtly he dropped in two quotations, one from Aratus and another from Cleanthes, two Greek poets popular at that time. In doing so he said, "I'm not just some country bumpkin from out of town. I am not peddling foreign or outmoded ideas. I know something about your world. I've read what you've read and studied what you've studied. I am making a point that any well-read Athenian should know. I teach about the God of whom your own experts speak!"

We see the culminating beauty of Paul's pedagogic symphony when we hear the thunderous applause at the conclusion. Actually, it might not sound like thunderous applause to some of us, but I think Paul might have heard it ring pleasantly in his ears.

We have to consider who his students were. These were third-degree pagans. At least, that's the term I use for them. First-degree nonbelievers are those people who don't believe because it has never crossed their mind that they should believe in anything. Second-degree nonbelievers are those people who have made a halfhearted attempt to commit to some alternatives. They know they aren't Christians, but they don't know why. Then we have third-degree nonbelievers, those people who are blatant in their attacks on Christians and are spokespersons for the alternative.

These philosophers in Paul's class were leaders of the third-degree faction. They were the pagan theologists. They wrote the books and preached the sermons and told the masses that if they didn't believe as the scholars believed, they were wrong. They made their living being pagans.

With his lesson, Paul challenged the very foundation of their faith. It is obvious he shook them out of their comfort zones. They weren't so sure anymore. Some went so far as to risk all their religious heritage by wanting to hear more. And some even became believers! Thunderous approval for sure and a resounding endorsement of an artistically developed lesson.

Chapter 17

Tell Me a Story

Matthew, Mark, Luke

"The kingdom of heaven is like treasure hidden in a field."

Matthew 13:44

"Two thousand years after Jesus delivered his lessons, people are still quoting him. I call that effective teaching."

197

 Jesus taught in parables. We all know that. At the very mention of Jesus as Master Teacher, people will nod their heads and say, "Yes, he taught in parables." Even those with just a smattering of Bible knowledge not only know about the parables, but occasionaly drop little references into their conversations to make their points more clearly and emphatically. "Well, as you know, every family has at least one prodigal son!" "I tried to warn the boss about that, but it was like scattering seed on rocky soil." "When my opportunity comes, I want to have my lamp trimmed and full of oil." "They have a good team this year, but they still have to go out to the highways and hedges to compel people to come to the games."

Two thousand years after Jesus delivered his lessons, people who aren't that interested in the theme of the lesson are still quoting the language and alluding to the image. I call that effective teaching.

You have probably been looking for this chapter from the time you started reading the book. "If this is a book about teaching strategies in the Bible, where is the chapter on the parables of Jesus? Everyone agrees that he taught deep truths and lasting lessons from little stories of everyday life."

There are three reasons why I have placed this chapter toward the end of the book. First, I suspected that you were expecting it. You already know that the parables have much to teach about methodology. Before we came to this obvious point, I wanted you to look at some other teaching examples that you may not have not considered before.

The second reason I have put this chapter here is that it is something of a summary of the earlier points. In the parables, Jesus masterfully incorporated many excellent teaching methods. Simply but effectively, he illustrated for us many of the strategies that famous teachers throughout history claimed to have discovered on their own. Because we have already discussed some of those strategies, this chapter serves as a review.

The third reason for positioning this chapter near the end is that I want you to finish the book with a bang. I want you to come to two conclusions that not only inform but inspire. First, we can all learn something about effective teaching by studying the Bible and concluding that we can implement these principles in our own teaching to accomplish our goal of becoming the best teachers we can possibly be. As an example, let's look at some of the specific pointers we can gather from analyzing the Master Teacher at work.

From the Known to the Unknown.

"Start where your students are," the educational experts tell us as they are trying to teach us a newly discovered principle of human learning. "Before you start the main part of your lesson, find out where they are—what they have stored in their learning banks, what thoughts and ideas and experiences they have brought to the process of comprehending the depth of your material." That is good advice, and our students surely appreciate our applying it, but it isn't all that new. Starting where your students are is precisely what Jesus did when he taught in parables.

Regardless of how many students he had in class, regardless of what their careers were, regardless of their stations in life, Jesus always had a little story right off the page of their experience. I am sure he won their attention with the story. I am sure he even won their interest with the story. But the story accomplished another purpose: he won their mental participation.

To understand how this works, let's establish a principle of storytelling. The good story is not the one I tell, but the one you tell yourself while I am telling my story—the story you remember as soon as I start mine—the story you already have in your memory bank. That's the story you will remember after we have finished the lesson and you are pausing to let it sink in.

Jesus told his students stories. He told stories about farming and farm life. He told stories about families and family relationships. He told stories about big events such as weddings. He told stories about land owners and tenants. He told stories about bosses and employees. In his parables, he included everyone.

Can you picture Jesus standing in the midst of a group of shepherds talking about a little sheep wandering off? Don't you imagine they slapped their knees and chuckled and told people nearby, "I once looked for a critter for ten hours—found him behind a rock."

Can you imagine a distraught parent sitting on the edge of a log trying to catch all the details about another father whose son left home?

These are real-life experiences. These are the stories that we know. Once we have heard these stories and have added our own application and embellishments, we are ready to move to the part of the lesson that we haven't experienced—to the unknown.

Obviously, we won't be able to start every class by finding one little story that will strike a relevant chord with every student, but the principle is still a powerful insight worthy of our consideration and our effort.

Finding that right story just once is like discovering a precious gem in your backyard. When you see the expression in their faces, the glint in their eyes that tells you that they are not just listening with their ears but with their hearts, the willingness with which they move from the known to the deeper point of the lesson—once you have seen all that, you'll keep digging for the rest of your career just hoping that you might be able to find another precious gem just like that last one.

Move From the Concrete to the Abstract.

My friend told of the time she held her three-year-old granddaughter. "Grandma, I have Jesus in my heart," the little one announced.

"That's wonderful!" Grandmother exclaimed. "But how do you know that?"

"If you hold your hand up here, you can feel him jump," the little girl assured her.

Actually, I like that theology. Having Jesus should make your heart jump. The little girl was expressing what many of us have felt. Unfortunately, though, she had missed the point. She was trying to squeeze an abstract idea into a concrete mind, and her difficulty in comprehending explains one of the major problems in teaching the Christian faith.

To borrow a line from Paul, I know in whom I believe. I know him well—his character, his attributes, his presence; but I don't have the language skills to give a physical description clear enough to draw you a picture.

In John 21, the disciples had not caught any fish until Jesus told them to throw their nets on the other side of the boat. Then they caught 153 big ones. I know why they caught those fish, but I can't explain it satisfactorily to an unbeliever.

So how did the Master Teacher teach an abstract concept to a concrete mind? He used parables. He started with a concrete description of a concrete situation. Once he had his students' minds focused, he could help them jump all the way from the concrete to the abstract.

God's love is an abstract idea, one that strains the comprehension of even the most devout believer. How do we squeeze the reality of God's love into the fixed parameters of human thoughts? By using a comprehendable concept, such as "father." I can describe a loving father to my students well enough that they can sense, they can feel the relationship. Then, when I direct their thoughts to the father who joyfully and completely forgave his wayward son, I can encourage them to stretch their perception of fatherhood into the realm of the abstract where they truly feel God's love.

With the parables, Jesus brought his students from the concrete to the abstract. As teachers, we understand that this is the task before us. We know the task is of great significance, but also know how hard it is to accomplish. That's why we study the parables carefully to see if we can find a clue that may help us be the agent that helps one person jump the chasm between concrete thinking and abstract thinking.

Place the Responsibility on the Learner.

Jesus taught in parables. He told the story, drew the lesson from the story, and then went on to his next mission. He didn't stick around prying and prodding to see who got the point. On a couple of occasions he did stop and offer a little explanation to the disciples, but you can tell from his reaction that he wanted his learners to work at the meaning themselves.

I am sure his students made those little comments we often hear:

- "This is hard."
- "We've never had to do this before."
- "Our teacher last year explained it better than you do."
- "Is this going to be on the test?"
- "Why don't you just tell us what you want us to know?"
- "I can't do this, and it's all your fault."

Jesus didn't listen to their complaints. Some learning is hard, and the more important lessons can be downright painful. Frequently, the kind of growth in character that Jesus was after caused discomfort in his students. That kind of change requires the student to take a long, hard look at his heart and his motives. Then the student just may have to chip away a few rough edges and unruly pieces. This is hard work, and it hurts. Life-changing lessons are frequently painful.

We teachers, regardless of how good we may be, can't grow and change for our students. They have to do it on their own. Jesus taught the parable, but he expected the students to do their part. We learn from Scripture that some of his students didn't do their part. They didn't come to the lesson with their defenses down and their vulnerability showing, or with the willingness to chip away at their own hearts—and they didn't learn the lesson. Jesus wept for them, but he let the lesson stand.

One of the most discouraging realities of teaching is that some of our students aren't ready—or willing—to learn. Not yet! We can stay up late at night and prepare. We can pray. We can weep for them. All we can do is do our best, lesson after lesson believing that someday the students will discover the willingness to learn, and the stories we tell now will still be in their memory bank.

So there you have it. You now know all there is to know about the Master Teacher teaching through parables! Of course you don't, and neither do I. There are too many lessons, too many implications, too many profound insights for us ever to think that we have mastered all of the message of Jesus' teaching through parables. If we study the rest of our lives, we won't even come close. But that is the truly wonderful reality of this method. Regardless of how many times we have read one of the parables, every time we read it again we can expect a new insight, a new twist, a new revelation. With that learning, we will more clearly comprehend the kingdom of God, and that will make us more effective children and more effective teachers.

Chapter 18

The Teacher
as the Student

Mark 10:13-16

"I tell you the truth, anyone who will not receive the kingdom of God like a little child will never enter it."

Mark 10:15

"We have all sorts of instructional sources—including those wonderful people God put in our classes."

209

As many college students do, my student Mark has a part-time job and a limited budget. However, every Saturday afternoon he gathers the money he has managed to save during the week, buys sandwich material, travels to that part of the city where the homeless hang out, and spends his Saturday evening offering sandwiches and the gospel to street people. I found that out by accident.

"It's just something I like to do," Mark responded when I asked him. " I don't want to call attention to myself."

Every time I look at Mark, I am reminded that Jesus washed the disciples' feet. The Son of God came to earth to serve, and as his children we also ought to wash each other's feet.

"Who is the best teacher you have ever had?" I asked a junior high youth group, expecting a wide range of answers from the kindergarten teacher who hugged them to the fifth grade teacher who visited them when they were sick.

"My dad," two students, a brother and a sister, yelled back in unison.

"What do you mean, your dad?" I asked.

"Oh, during daily devotions at our house, he doesn't just read the Bible story. He acts it out and talks with accents and makes the characters seem so real. He's great.

Daily devotions are big at our house," those students told me.

Their answer took me by surprise because their dad is a student in my college class. He is a quiet man who sits near the back. He never volunteers to speak, and when I call on him, he answers in a halting style that indicates his natural shyness.

Every time I look at him I am reminded that my first teaching responsibility assigned to me by the authority of Scripture is to my own family.

My student Helen is planning a career as an elementary school teacher when she finishes college next year. Helen is fifty-seven years old. Every time I look at her I am reminded that Jesus gives us the abundant life, but we have to throw in a little effort ourselves, regardless of our age or circumstances.

Recently, I was trying to get a high school class into a discussion—not for some noble teaching purpose but because I had finished the lesson ten minutes early! I had to come up with something to keep those adolescents from acting adolescent until the bell rescued us all.

"Who is your favorite Bible character?" I shouted over the din.

"John Mark," came back a rather strange response.

211

"John Mark?" I asked with a bit of shock in my voice.

"Sure," the young theologian instructed me in typical teenage picturesque speech. "When old Paul dissed him, he didn't freak. He just chilled out. Cool man."

I don't know how those adolescents spent their Sunday afternoon, but I spent mine pleasantly pondering how that story must have developed. At one time, Paul was adamant about his displeasure with John Mark. In fact, his displeasure was so strong that it caused him and Barnabas to go their separate ways (Acts 15:36-41). Years later, however, when Paul was in prison in Rome, his estimation of John Mark was quite different. To Timothy he requested, "Get Mark and bring him with you, because he is helpful to me in my ministry" (2 Timothy 4:11).

Obviously, Paul and John Mark had reconciled. How did their reconciliation come about? Which one made the first move? What were the steps in the procedure? We don't know any of that information, of course, but I really enjoyed the afternoon I spent in Bible study because of that young man's observation. Every time I read about John Mark, I recall how I was taught by a group of teens that I was simply trying to corral.

The Carrs, a couple in my class, are rather calm people who usually don't attract much attention. Two years ago another high school student attacked their son and the injuries were serious enough to require medical attention. That evening the Carrs made a surprise visit to the parents of the other boy. They did not go with malice in their hearts. They are not that kind of people. They went with compassion, and that night both of the parents of the other boy committed their hearts and lives to Jesus. Every time I look at the Carrs, I am reminded of what Jesus said about forgiving others.

Carl, a middle-aged student in my class, reads the Bible through from cover to cover every year. He advocates this method of study. He says that it helps him see the whole story, but he also says that every time he goes through it he sees deep truths in passages that he doesn't hear about otherwise.

I can attest to the success of his reading method because he is invaluable in helping the rest of us find study passages. He should know where they are—he has been reading the Bible through every year for the past twenty-one years. Ever since I have known Carl, my Bible study habits have changed. Because of the example of this student of mine, I now read through God's Word, cover-to-cover, every year.

I could go on forever. There are countless lessons I have learned from those whom I was supposed to be teaching.

Years ago when I was young, impetuous, and inexperienced, I envisioned my job as that of a Christian guru. I would spout wisdom and my learners would soak it in. I saw teaching as a one-way experience.

I have learned something since then. It is the lesson Jesus taught the day he left the disciples on usher duty. "People were bringing little children to Jesus to have him touch them, but the disciples rebuked them" (Mark 10:13).

Surely the disciples meant well. The Master Teacher was surely teaching some profound lesson. He didn't have time to bother with a bunch of children running and squirming. He had to give adults the answers to the questions of life. Let Jesus teach the parents and then let them go home and teach these children what they had learned.

Jesus countered that idea, however. He paused to demonstrate that children weren't merely secondary learners. They were potential teachers. Jesus welcomed the children and allowed their innocent, trusting, seeking behavior to teach life-hardened adults by example.

Of course, we teachers are models of Christian living for our students regardless of whether we teach five year olds or eighty year olds. At the same time, we need to remember that we are learners, too. While they are learning from us, we learn from them.

I don't know all the qualities Jesus saw in those children that he wants us to imitate, but it is fun to attempt to construct the list: innocence, genuineness, the ability to forgive and forget—all those child-like qualities of faith. But add to that list the willingness to learn, the eagerness to grow.

Every day we are reminded afresh that we are like children just starting on the great adventure of life; God is not finished with us yet. There is so much ahead of us to learn—facts to find, insights yet to comprehend, talents and gifts yet to be discovered. One of the great joys of life is the excitement of getting up every morning and saying, "I am going to learn something today." As teachers, we have all sorts of instructional sources—books, seminars, and those wonderful people that God chose to put in our classes.

The other day Will, a three-year-old philosopher I know, came to me and said, "Grandpa, teach me how to tie my shoes." No false pride. No one-upmanship games to prove which one of us was the more knowledgeable. No barriers. No resistance. Just a pure, innocent learning situation.

I think that is part of what Jesus was trying to tell us that day. That's the attitude we take to class with us. Maybe students will learn something today, but I know I will. That's why I am so excited about this calling to teach—not only because of what I might give them but because of what I know I will receive.

Chapter 19

The Ultimate Resource

James 1:5

"If any of you lacks wisdom, he should ask God."

James 1:5

"The task of teaching is too overwhelming and the impact too significant for us not to claim the promise Jesus made to us."

- Should I read the quotation from Vance Havener before I have them get into groups or after?
- I explained the idea twice, but their eyes tell me that some understand and some of them don't. Should I explain it again and risk boring those who got the point for the sake of those who didn't?
- Mrs. Anderson is having surgery this week. Should I use that illustration about the author who died on the operating table? It is really appropriate to my point, but I don't want to upset her.
- The Smith's youngest daughter left for college this week. Do I have time to stop by the store and get a card, or is it not that important?
- Jared is leaning back in his chair. I'm afraid he might fall, but is it worth stopping the whole class to tell him to quit?
- Karen is only in the ninth grade, but she is already so boy crazy. Dangerously so! I'm really worried about her. Should I talk to her parents?
- How important is it to have these kids memorize the books of the Bible? Every year, the protests get louder and louder, and they more are reluctant to do it. Maybe I should just cancel that requirement.
- Oh, no! I forgot to look on the map to find out where Bithynia

is. Is that really important enough for me to get out of bed and look it up before tomorrow's lesson?

- How do I respond when Suzanne gives me that stare? Does she really hate me or am I reading something into it?
- Which literature should we order for next year?

Decisions! Decisions! Decisions! Decisions!

Teaching is about making decisions. The quality of our teaching depends on the decisions we make. When we make good decisions, we teach effectively. When we make bad decisions, our effectiveness suffers the consequences.

Not only do decision-demanding situations come in bunches and in a variety of shapes and kinds, but they also come rapidly and often with a sense of urgency. Have you ever wished you could just stop the action, go home and sleep on it, and come back tomorrow refreshed with the confidence of reflection so that you could make a better decision? Too often, it doesn't work that way. We are forced by the situation to make a decision and take action right now. I call those the "flat forehead moments" because I go home, replay the whole incident, slap my forehead with my open palm and say, "Oh, now I know what I should have done."

The really frightening reality is that our decisions have consequences. We could fill a book with stories from people of all ages who were permanently scarred or permanently blessed by a decision a teacher once made on the spur of the moment.

One of the major cautions that comes with the call to teach is to know we are not wise enough to make all those decisions well, and to make them under the stress of urgency with which they come. But we do know the One who is wise enough, and we have his wonderful promise that if we humbly ask, he will share his wisdom with us. I call James 1:5 the teacher's verse because I have no idea how we could ever venture to accept the stricter judgment promised us without the full assurance that we have the promise of God's wisdom available at the moment of every decision. I have copies of that verse pasted everywhere—on my bathroom mirror, on the flyleaf of my Bible, on the cover of my plan book, and on the lectern in the classroom. I never want to be too far away from it.

The first step of lesson preparation is to pray for wisdom. The last step, after we have found all the notes, opened our Bible to the appropriate spot, spit out our gum, and checked the clothes to make sure we're buttoned and zipped, and stepped to the front of the class, is to pray again for wisdom.

The task of teaching is too overwhelming and the impact too significant for us not to claim the promise Jesus made to us. We are not wise enough to do this by ourselves. We must accept God's offer to work through us when we accept the role of being his agents.

We have a whole tub of resources to provide us both instruction and inspiration—seminars, film series, banquets, books, and journals. But nothing has a more powerful effect on our teaching confidence than to find ourselves suddenly making with a decision in a stressful situation, which we were not bright enough to make, but finding that we made a good decision. In the calm that follows we ask, "Where did that come from? How did I know to do that?"

We do the best we can. We read the material and research the background. We search our minds for techniques of presentation, we think through the lesson from beginning to end. We find the energy to be enthusiastic. That's the least we can do.

When we have done all we can do, we remind ourselves that if we teach for Jesus and that if we humbly and faithfully ask for wisdom, we never work alone!